Jay for Kidz

by

Jason Fernandez

Bloomington, IN Milton Keynes, UK

authorHOUSE

AuthorHouse™
1663 Liberty Drive, Suite 200
Bloomington, IN 47403
www.authorhouse.com
Phone: 1-800-839-8640

AuthorHouse™ UK Ltd.
500 Avebury Boulevard
Central Milton Keynes, MK9 2BE
www.authorhouse.co.uk
Phone: 08001974150

This book is a work of non-fiction. Unless otherwise noted, the author and the publisher make no explicit guarantees as to the accuracy of the information contained in this book and in some cases, names of people and places have been altered to protect their privacy.

First published by AuthorHouse 9/14/2006

ISBN: 1-4259-2273-2 (sc)

Printed in the United States of America
Bloomington, Indiana

This book is printed on acid-free paper.

Contents

Introduction

This will be a book like no other you have read. I will try to help you understand this crazy and confusing world today's youth are living in. Your generation has many challenges and difficulties to overcome. I will attempt to give you a guide to help you understand and make better decisions now that will greatly affect your future. I will not sugarcoat any of my views or beliefs. I will not tell you what to do or with whom to hang or what choices you should make. I only want you take my advice and try to look at the world for what it really is. I will be talking to you straight from my heart and using my experiences to, hopefully, help your experiences be more fulfilling and exciting.

I may swear or become angry, but let's face it, you have already heard the words I may use. I want to be clear on a few things before I get into telling you what I have been through. I am not a writer; I have never written a book before. I have lived a troubled life and have learned many things. Some of my experiences I wish to forget and some have changed the way I think and who I am forever. I want you to understand that every action, decision, or choice you make can dramatically change you as well. Other things will happen to you that are unable to be controlled. All you can do is build up your strength and, with a bit of luck, learn from life. It is never too late to try new things or begin new friendships or become closer to relatives in your life.

Okay, let's get on to some good shit........

Why I feel I can help you

My name is Jason Fernandez. I was born in Manchester, Connecticut, July 15, 1977. My mother, Gale Wilcox, and father, Joseph Fernandez II, were raised in a middle- to lower-class setting. They were married at the ages of thirty-two and thirty-six respectively. From there, they set out to raise a family and their quality of life. My father and uncle had bought a small auto body garage on the Berlin Turnpike in Newington, Connecticut during the 1960s. My uncle was very good at fixing cars and my father was a smart businessman. Together, they made it work. Business was rolling in and so was the money.

By the year 1975, my mother gave birth to my older brother, Joseph Fernandez III. They lived in a new house my father had constructed. It sat on a small hill at the end of a dead-end road in Wethersfield, Connecticut. Wethersfield is considered to be a wealthy town with excellent schools and very little crime. The town was proud of this considering that Hartford, Connecticut, was the next town over. In 1977, my mother again became pregnant, with me. All seemed well for the Fernandez family: one son and another on the way, a big, beautiful home in a rich neighborhood. It was the American dream right?…Wrong!

Before I was even born, my first major life lesson was playing out. My father, who enjoyed riding ten-speed bicycles for exercise, was on his usual route when a boy made a move towards the road. An older woman became scared and swerved completely over to the other side of the road and struck my father head-on. To make things worse, my father had strapped his feet to his peddles to get more power out of the bike. When the car hit him, the bike went under the car and he went over. As his feet were strapped in, he actually broke right out of his shoes. With his shoes still attached to the bike, he flew over the car and landed on the other side. He broke nearly eighty percent of the bones in his body and his left leg lay barely attached. Somehow, he managed to hang on.

Clinging to life in the emergency room, he pulled through. But there was a price to pay for survival. My father was paralyzed from the waist down and would spend the next two years of his life in a full-body cast. In the blink of an eye, the Fernandez family would never be the same. My father was in the hospital when I was born. He was unable to tell my mother how happy he was to see me because most of his teeth were missing. When I was two years old, my father was released from the hospital. He would need to use crutches for the rest of his life to get around. My father decided to make it easier on himself and had an elevator installed in our house. Before I was old enough to realize why I had an elevator in my house, I thought it was cool.

The next few years that followed were difficult for my mother. She tried to take care of my father the best she could, but he was a changed man now and not the person she had fallen in love with. At the same time, my uncle made some decisions at the auto body shop that would begin to push my father out, and he would become sole owner of the business they had built together. To this day, I still do not really know how or why this happened, but in the end, it did.

When I was six and my brother was eight, my mother pulled me aside and tried to tell me that she was getting a divorce. I really didn't know what the hell she was talking about. It was not as if I could have done anything about it anyway. My father sold our house for $450,000 in 1983. He purchased a small condo in Wethersfield and some beat-up apartment buildings in Middletown, Connecticut. My mother moved my brother and me into another condo she rented in Wethersfield as well. I guess they wanted us to remain in the Wethersfield school system. My mother had custody of us, and we were able to spend two weekends a month with my father. He was beginning to move around better and spent his time fixing up the apartments he bought in Middletown. My mother went back to her old job at Northeast Utilities in the payroll department. She had a high school diploma which limited the amount of money she made. My bother and I remained enrolled at Corpus Christi Catholic School. We had to wear uniforms and some of our teachers were nuns. I think I can say, in third grade, a year or two after the divorce, my attitude changed.

My first order of business was to find some other boys who were as pissed off as I was. No problem. I found two buddies who were ready to raise hell alongside me. Hey, let's face it, having some people getting in trouble with you makes you feel as if you're not alone. We began by targeting a few kids in school and kicking their asses whenever we could. We would make fun of them until they cried. In class, at recess, whenever an opportunity came up to make them feel like shit, we took it. We ended up spending a lot of time in the principal's office and many parents complained. We loved it. At the time, we thought we were the coolest kids in our class. The other boys and girls all seemed to like us and did what we asked them to do. Looking back, I think all of the other kids were afraid of us and felt if they were nice to us, we would not pick on them. Whatever the case, it didn't matter, we enjoyed all of the attention. This went on for two more years. During this time, some of the kids we picked on had older brothers who would try and defend them without success. My one friend was big for his age and would take care of them quickly. I remember a time in fifth grade, a high school freshman was walking by my school and my friend and I beat him up just to see if we could.

My brother was still pretty calm during all this but his anger was building. By the end of fifth grade, the school had had enough. I was expelled and started six grade in public school. The first thing I did was seek out the troublemakers and become their friend. At this point, I was also becoming interested in girls. It was the first time I didn't have to see a girl in their same old boring uniform. I was in heaven. My brother remained at the Catholic school. Again, I would terrorize teachers and any other kids I did not think were cool. Of course, the other students all seemed to like me. Girls wanted my approval and guys wanted to be seen hanging out with me. The teachers hated me. They moved me into two separate classrooms trying to separate me from my friends. I was able to continue to cause trouble by making new friends and picking on different kids. By the end of the year, my grades were horrible and I was moved into the special education class. There were only five of us, and keeping us under control was the objective, not teaching.

My mother continued to struggle to support us. My father was able to give us child support and money my uncle was paying him to buy him out of the business all together. We would spend two of our weekends a month with him and ride ten-speed bikes as he once did. My brother and I both were able to vent anger in a positive way competing in cycling races and practicing after school. My mother worked long hours and most of the time, we went to an after-school daycare center at some lady's house in Wethersfield. Her idea of daycare was sitting in front of the television as the kids ran wild in the back yard unsupervised for hours on end.

All the overtime work my mother did allowed her to purchase a townhouse a half-hour drive away in Meriden, Connecticut. Still, she wanted us to remain in Wethersfield schools. Since my father still lived in Wethersfield, we lied and said we lived with him so we could. The problem with living in one town and going to school in another was I had no friends in Meriden and no way to see my friends in Wethersfield outside school. This increased the anger in my brother and me. At this point, I was just entering the middle school. The school was much bigger and there were many more kids to pick on and get in trouble with. This was where I met some of the people I am still in contact with today. I became friends with the kids who were poor students and hated school. We would wander the halls and try to avoid class. We were still well liked by the girls and guys and they would always be hanging out with us. We tried to stay up on all the latest music and fashions and concentrated on dancing. During our middle school dances, we would open up circles and entertain the other students with our moves. To the mind of a troubled seventh grader, this was what life was about: acting cool, having friends, getting suspended, disobeying teachers and parents, no matter what the cost.

At the same time, my brother was entering high school. It was a big change for him since he remained at the Catholic school until this point. Wethersfield High had about 1200 students enrolled. My brother loved it at first. He also found some troublemakers and introduced them to me. He could not hang out with them after school because of where we lived, so he began to cut class and leave the school with them. They would go to a friend's house when the parents were at work and smoke pot. By the time my brother was sixteen, he was a high school dropout staying home every day watching television and smoking weed.

By the summer of my eighth grade year, my grades were so poor I had to attend summer school in order to graduate to high school. Of course, I thought I was too cool for that so I did not attend. Both of my parents were beginning to realize that my brother and I were heading for a world of shit. They tried to help us, but my mother was working and involved with an alcoholic boyfriend who would make her crazy at times. She would take her frustrations out on us, only pushing us further away. By the end of the summer, I was told I had to repeat the eighth grade. The first week, I got into a couple fights picking on the new kids in the school. I was suspended for a week. When I returned to school, I was told they did not want to deal with me for a whole other year and sat me in the library, making me do the work I missed in summer school. Within two weeks, they bumped me up to high school as a ninth grader. The next four years of my life would change me forever.

As a freshman in high school, I immediately found myself hanging out with the older kids who also came from broken homes. It seemed as if we all had something in common. We hated life. We felt as if someone owed us something and we were going to piss people off until we got it.

In 1990, the same year I was starting in high school, my mother moved us back to Wethersfield. We bought a house a quarter mile away from the school. It would be the first time in years that I would be able to hang out with friends after school and on the weekends. I would wake up in the morning trying to not wake my brother who was usually stoned out of his mind and walk over to the high school. I would grab a few of my buddies and walk right back out. We would take what little lunch money we had and walk down to a cigarette machine and get some smokes. We would then cruise around town causing trouble until we got bored and went to my house. It was perfect, my mother was at work until 4:00 and the kids could easily walk back to the school by 2:00 to catch the bus. When the high school would call us into the office for skipping school, they would punish us by suspending us for ten days each. We thought, shit, now I am excused from school for ten days. I did not see this as a punishment, but a gift.

By the middle of my freshman year, there were about thirty of us kids who were out of school hanging out daily. We separated ourselves from the other kids by wearing Raiders football jackets. Every day at 2:00, we would all walk from my house and stand across the street from the high school waiting for anyone to say anything wrong to us. If a child's parents bought them a Raiders coat and they had the balls to wear it, we took it from them by force. We thought we were the shit.

As parents drove by with their kids, they would point over and say, "You see those boys over there? They are losers. I do not ever want to see you hanging out with them."

By the end of my freshman year, the town was mandated to have me in school because I was only fourteen years old. They sent me to an elementary school across town that had one classroom being used for remedial students and troublemakers. We would spend most of the day playing volleyball and watching television. I fit right in with these kids. I did not stay long. My friends who had cars would cruise the streets of other neighborhoods looking for kids to jump. We would go by other high schools and look for kids wearing Raiders coats and beat them up. Sometimes, we would just beat them up because we did not like the way they looked at us.

By February of the first year living back in Wethersfield, I had been arrested about eight times including assault, disorderly conduct, possession of a deadly weapon, assault with a deadly weapon, and numerous charges of breach of peace. I was beginning to build up quite a reputation with the police and community. They placed me on juvenile probation and monitored me monthly. In February of 1991, I chased a boy down the street with a BB gun threatening to shoot him. He, of course, thought the gun was real and probably shit his pants trying to get away. When I was arrested this time, I was waiting for my mother to get me as usual. She never came.

The police took me to Hartford Detention Center in Shackles. The center was located on the corner of Park Street and Broad Street, right in the heart of Hartford's toughest neighborhood. My first night there, I broke down. I was scared and alone. I did not have any of my friends to protect me and these kids looked rough. For the next two weeks, I remained incarcerated. Kids who were the size of grown men would kick the shit out of each other over any reason they could think of. I remained quiet and tried to mind my own business. My strategy worked and I somehow made it out of there unharmed.

Back on the streets, I was more pissed off than ever. I began smoking pot every day and remained out of school. I would find friends to get high with all day long and smoke with my brother at night. My mother would come home from work and pass out. She had no clue what was going on. My relationship with my Dad was barely there. He was doing all he could to survive and so was I. Having him not in the house made it hard for him to punish me. How can you enforce rules when you cannot see if they are being followed?

By October of 1992, I was fifteen years old and a high-school dropout. The school was in charge of educating me until the age of sixteen. That month, the court system told my mother they were taking me to a juvenile facility located one hour away in Litchfield, Connecticut. I was placed on juvenile parole for twenty-four months. Depending on my behavior, I could be away for two years. Who's cool now? This facility had been around for about one hundred years. It held eighty-two of Connecticut's best. There was one other place for kids in the state that was worse. I was lucky enough to avoid seeing the inside of it. During my stay at the

Connecticut Junior Republic, I began to discover sports again. I became involved in woodworking and going to school. The counselors gave me a new outlook on life. The boys could get physical at times, but I was used to it and fought back when needed. I remained at CJR for fourteen months. I had matured and began, for the first time, to see I had many more talents than bullying others, hanging out on the streets, and talking to girls. I was able to get my driver's license before I left. My mother and father bought me a used car right before I returned home. November 4th 1993, I will never forget that date. I was back in Wethersfield, no criminal record, armed with a car and valid license. The last time I drove was when I was fourteen and we would steal my mother's car at night to go get weed in Hartford.

It wasn't long before the Wethersfield police knew my car and would pull me over every chance they got. Within the first year of having my car, I received three speeding tickets, two reckless driving tickets, and a few for running a red light. Finally, my license was suspended when my friends and I saw this kid we did not like and I drove up next to him and hit him with my car, breaking his leg. I was arrested again for assault with a deadly weapon, reckless driving, and felony assault. Since I was over the age of sixteen, I was no longer a juvenile and was sent to adult court. I was able to use what is called a Y.O. or youthful offender and get it cleared off my record. I ignored the suspension and continued to drive to school.

My friends were beginning to change; I started to hang out with the kids in school who liked drugs. We attended class and kept our grades up, but on the weekends, we would drink beer and experiment with acid and mushrooms. These powerful drugs would make us paranoid and we would bug out for hours not knowing where we were or what may happen to us. By my senior year of high school, my brother decided to get his shit together and got his GED He left home and went to a small college in Vermont. I continued to smoke pot and began to sell drugs to other kids in town. Parents and police in the town knew what I was up to and my reputation as a bad kid continued. What I learned in CJR was slipping away and drugs were taking over.

Halloween of my senior year, I attended the high school dance. My friends and I decided to get drunk before we went. As I did in the past, I opened up a dance circle in the crowd. At the time, there were pumpkins on the floor smashed. I decided to move them so we did not slip. I did this by kicking them out of the circle. The police who were in charge of security at the dance and who knew me from the past felt I was trying to hurt people with the pumpkins. Before I could understand what was going on, three officers tackled me into a table where they put mace in my eyes and smashed their knees into my face. I tried to fight back and they only pushed harder. As my entire school watched, I was placed in handcuffs and dragged out of the dance bleeding and unable to see. I spent the next four days in the Wethersfield holding cell on a cement block. The police charged me with assault on a police officer, breach of peace, and disorderly conduct. I guess this was their way of making an example of me in front of the other students. When parents and the community read the article in the newspaper about it, I am sure they cheered. I left the police station fucked up and seriously pissed off. I returned to school the next day and the other kids could not believe what had happened.

A few weeks later, a friend of mine was staying in Florida with his family. While we were drunk and screwed up on valium, my female friend and I thought it would be a good idea to pay him a visit. Heading down Highway 95 South, we took a detour to Washington, D.C. to check out the sights. It was about 3:00 a.m. at the time. We parked the car next to the Washington Monument and had a beer. I noticed it was very dark and there were a lot of cars parked. I began to look through the windows for money or something to steal. In one car, I saw a briefcase and what looked to be a wallet. The car was locked. I went back and found a screwdriver in the trunk of our car and broke the window out. As I looked up, I saw a police monkey light shining in my eyes. I immediately began to run towards the Lincoln Memorial. The girl who was driving the car took off in the other direction. The cop chased me on foot but I managed to hide under a large pine tree. For twenty minutes, I remained hidden. I watched as the number of police cars looking for me increased.

Soon, I heard loudspeakers from above telling me not to move. As I looked around, I saw flashlights coming towards me. I got up and ran again through a large field. A huge light was shining down on me when I realized a helicopter was chasing me. I continued to run towards the street. When I got to the sidewalk, two cop cars pulled out in front of me. I jumped over the hood and fell on the other side almost directly on a cop. They pinned me down and arrested me. I was charged with breaking and entering and destruction of property. In Maryland, the age of a juvenile was eighteen. I was only seventeen.

The next day, they transferred me to Virginia Juvenile Correction Facility. When I first arrived, the correction officer said, "Damn, we have not seen a white kid here in four years." This was a prison that held over one thousand inmates. They brought me in with about thirty other kids from the D.C. area. The first thing they make you do is take a shower butt-naked all together in one large room. As I looked at the other boys, I noticed almost every kid had large scars which looked as if they had been stabbed, and they had bullet wounds on their bodies. For the next two days, I remained in the unit for new prisoners. I contacted my mother and told her she or dad better get down here or I would not make it out alive. I hung on for two days using all the knowledge I had learned in the past being locked up to try and make some friends and keep my face in the shape it was before I went in. Finally, my mother drove down and paid my bail. I was released without any major damage. I returned with my father to court a week later and paid a fine for the vehicle's window. I have never returned to Washington, D.C.

When I returned home, I spoke several times to my brother at college in Vermont. He was beginning to convince me to try and take my SATs and go to college. My grades were poor, and as I missed so much school in the past, it was uncertain if I would graduate on time. I decided to take his advice. I enrolled in an SAT prep course after school and took my SATs and began applying to colleges. My results from the test were not great but I was able to do well enough to get accepted to a small Vermont college located in Castleton, Vermont. As I approached my high school graduation date, I was working hard to get all my work done. As the other seniors enjoyed three- and four-hour days and went to the beach, I was in class every day from eight a.m. to two p.m., only breaking for lunch. The week before I was to graduate, my vice principal, who did not like me one bit, called me in to tell me I was going to be one credit short and I could not graduate on time. I left her office crushed. Here I was making the effort to do something good and still I got no support. That day, I contacted Castleton State College in Vermont and told them what had happened. I asked if I were to drop out of school tomorrow and get my GED, if they would accept me; they agreed. The next day, I dropped out of high school six days short of graduation; it was 1995.

In July, I took the GED test and passed. By the end of the summer, I was preparing to leave for school in four days. I was finishing up my parole and was ready to go. As I was sitting in the police station talking to my parole officer, a cop approached me and said, "Been selling some LSD, Fernandez?" My heart almost stopped. Come to find out, a friend of mine had been arrested for possession of marijuana and had made a deal with the police to get me. A month earlier, I had sold him one hundred hits of LSD which he brought directly to the police. I was arrested again. This time, the charges were very serious. What made matters worse was that my house was so close to the high school that when I sold the drugs from my home, it was considered to be in a school zone. The police had a field day with the charges: Possession of LSD within 1500 feet of a school zone, sale of LSD within 1500 feet of a school zone, risk of injury to minors, operating a drug factory within 1500 feet of a school zone. If convicted on all counts, I could face life in prison. I sat again in the Wethersfield holding cell and waited two days for court. My mother could not afford a lawyer so I was on my own. I was two days from leaving for college and I was in jail again.

The morning of my court date, I was transferred to the New Britain, Connecticut holding cell, for people around the state who were waiting to be arraigned. There were about ten guys in there; I was the youngest. As I sat waiting for my turn, I noticed an inmate who was in a yellow state corrections jumpsuit and wearing leg shackles. He was looking around strangely as if sizing us up. I tried not to look at him and continued to talk to another inmate. The next thing I remember was sliding halfway down the wall of the cell; the guy in the jumpsuit was beating the shit out of my face. I tried to stop him but was unable to understand what was really happening. Moments later, an officer came in and grabbed the guy. Only then, did I begin to realize what had happened. Underneath my left eye was a large cut; my other one was beginning to swell shut. Both of my lips were cut and bleeding and blood was pouring from my nose. The guards pulled me from the cell and told me someone was going to have to take me to the hospital. I said I had been waiting to talk to the judge and that I was not going until I found out what was going to happen to me. For about ten minutes, I insisted I would go to the hospital only after seeing the judge; they agreed. As I approached the bench, my face looked as if I had been hit by a train. My shirt was covered in blood and so were my hands. I explained to the judge what had happened and my plans for college. He took sympathy on me and dropped three charges and only convicted me of possession of LSD within 1500 feet of a school zone. This was a felony charge that remains with me to this day. I was sentenced to three years in prison suspended on the grounds that I remain enrolled in college and not get arrested for three years.

Two days later, I was in Vermont, starting college with two black eyes and a bruised face. My brother had decided to transfer to the same school I was attending. During that first week of school, I was unable to find anyone who wanted to get into trouble. These kids seemed to be different from anyone I had ever hung around with. They all seemed to like school and wanted to learn. They talked about how they were excited to attend a certain class and how much they liked a certain professor. When I went over to visit some older students I had met, *Jeopardy* was on the television and most of them knew the answers. These kids didn't look like dorks to me, they were wearing baggy clothes, earrings in their ears; a few had some tattoos. Even one kid was sipping a beer. After a few weeks of hanging around with college students, I was beginning to realize that my idea of what I thought was cool was completely fucked up. These kids were thinking about their futures and goals they had set for themselves, places in the world they wanted to see, and what they wanted to get done during college. Most were not interested in drugs.

Before this point in my life, I had never looked at the world this way. I didn't see my environment as an open door that I could walk through if I made the effort to do so. I did not look to try and better myself. I always thought I needed to look like a tough guy in the eyes of others. I was consumed by always worrying what the person next to me thought of me. Were my clothes cool enough? Was my hair looking good? Do you think she likes me? To teenagers, these things are very important, and they should be. The way you express yourself is what identifies you to your friends. It gives you meaning. What you need to be careful of is letting what others think about you ruin you. What is cool to you now may not be so cool in the future. As you grow and mature, so will your ideas and values. People you meet and experiences you have will change your outlooks in life. It took me eighteen years of my life, and only after I removed myself from the place I grew up to realize this. At this point, my life again changed forever.

During my second week in college, I stopped doing drugs. I met the first person who helped to make me the man I am today. His name was Tim. He had just returned from a semester studying in Australia and had transferred to Castleton. He was funny, well spoken, easy to talk to, and very smart. Before him, I never thought to hang around with anyone smart or who wanted to learn about things. I used to rank on these people and call them geeks and losers. Tim was neither a geek nor a loser. Standing next to him, I was the loser. I felt embarrassed to talk about my past, so I didn't. I hung around with Tim, and he showed me how to write a college paper and study for a test. Every day, I would see him go to class, so I went to class. Before long, I was really looking up to him. Through him, I was again finding out that, hey, maybe I could be smart, too. I figured college could be another school to get in trouble at. I was wrong. Nobody in college made fun of each other; everyone was nice to the teachers. The school did not care whether or not you were in class, still everyone seemed to go. On the weekends, we would head out to a party and nobody was fighting.

The next six months, Tim, my brother, and I were always together. We enrolled in some of the same classes and liked all the same people. My grades were okay; it was difficult for me at first to get used to school. I had not cared for so long that I had missed a lot that was taught in high school. By the end of the first year, this feeling had passed. I was able to write a good paper and do well on tests. I found out that college wasn't really hard; it just took effort. At the end of my freshman year in college, three of us, Tim, my brother, and I rented a house on Lake Bomoseen near the school for the next school year. Tim went back to his hometown for the summer and my brother and I did not want to go back home. There was just too much trouble there. We had heard that Myrtle Beach, South Carolina, was a fun place to live. We packed our bags and a few hundred bucks and drove this piece-of-shit Volkswagen Jetta we had down there. Soon, we found some minimum-wage jobs and a cheap place to live. My brother worked as a line cook at Hooter's and I got a job busing tables at a restaurant called Dick's Last Resort. For the entire summer, we worked and cruised around. We were broke but managed to get by.

At the end of August, we returned to Vermont with no problems and a great life experience under our belt. My sophomore year in college, I continued to hang with Tim and my brother. I was still undecided in what I wanted to do for my major field of study. I decided to take a social work class and a juvenile justice class. The first week of both classes, I realized that I knew a lot about this shit. It almost came naturally to me. I had been involved in these situations personally. I could relate to what was being taught and figured that if I spoke up in class, I could maybe help others understand who had not been through what I had been through. Still, I was scared and embarrassed to do so. I kept to myself and pretended that I was just like every other kid in the class learning about this stuff for the first time. By the end of that year, I declared social work to be my major.

That summer, Tim, his girlfriend, my brother, and I decided we would try to go out to Santa Cruz, California, on a road trip and get some jobs and live. We took fifteen days to drive out, stopping at all the major southern sites: the Rocky Mountains, Grand Canyon, Las Vegas, the Hoover Dam. We then ended up in Santa Cruz and found a house that had thirty or so other kids our age living it. It was called a co-op or community house that was completely run by the kids living it. You were required to work at the house doing chores for five hours a week. You and three others would have to prepare dinner for the entire house one night a week. The rent was cheap and you were able to pay month-by-month. All four of us quickly found cheesy little jobs. My brother and I worked in a surf shop. Tim was a waiter at a convalescent home. His girl worked at a bagel shop. Again, the summer was spent working, meeting new people, and having fun. On the way home, we went north and saw Yellowstone, Craters of the Moon State Park, Mount Rushmore, the Mississippi River, and the Saint Louis Arch. I learned more about life and this beautiful country we live in on that trip.

During my third year in college, I became more involved in social work. I had built a small relationship with a few of the professors. They said they were excited to have me in the program and encouraged me to stick with it. I was beginning to feel proud of my work. This pushed me only to work harder and put more effort into my studies. By the end of the year, my good friend Tim was getting ready to graduate, and my brother was planning to move in with his new girlfriend. I also moved in with my new girlfriend down the street. I spent that summer working as a waiter in Manchester, Vermont. My last two years continued in this fashion. With every semester that passed, my grades continued to rise. Getting a C or lower had become out of the question. I was beginning to talk more about my past and using it to help others.

During my last year in college, I had doubled up my majors. I added a degree in sociology on to my workload. I was also completing a year-long internship at the Dismas House in Rutland, Vermont. It was a nonprofit halfway house for prisoners who were just getting out. I learned there that prisoners without some assistance when they leave are almost certain to return to jail. When a prisoner is released, the state buys them a bus ticket and says good luck. Most have nowhere to go and no money to start a new life and end up committing a crime to try and survive. This cycle may continue throughout their lives. The Dismas House allowed for some support and structure to assist them until they could make it on their own. I still cannot get over how taxpayers spend millions of dollars to house criminals, yet will not spend one dollar upon their release to help them remain free. It seems to me that our society wants to see these individuals fail at the expense of someone they victimize before they return.

In the summer of 2000, I had finished college and graduated with a degree in social work and a degree in sociology. I made it. Until this point, I had never successfully completed any school in my life.

A few days later, I was back in Wethersfield where it all began. I had a small graduation party and was already trying to think of how to get the hell out of town. I thought before I left I would call up the Connecticut Junior Republic where I was sent as a teenager and tell them what I had accomplished. I spoke with my old family worker who now had been promoted to director. He amazed me by asking me if I wanted a job as a counselor. At first, I thought, I can't do this. I had only gotten out of there six-and-a half-years ago. After a few more phone calls, he convinced me to give it a shot. A month out of college, I had made a full circle. I was placed in the exact same unit I had stayed in as a child. My old counselors were now my partners. Nothing had changed at the Republic. The same teachers and staff had remained. In its one-hundred-year history, you could count how many times a student had returned to work there. Four more years have passed and still I remain at the Connecticut Junior Republic. I am a youth counselor. I spend my days at work open about my past, using what I have learned to, hopefully, shed light on the world to kids there. I have worked with hundreds of boys just like me. It is hard for them to tell me, "You don't know what it is like to be where I am." I have been exactly where they are. I feel my accomplishments give hope to kids who, in their minds, have already given up. One of my favorite sayings is: "Being down is good...you have nowhere else to go but up."

I cannot say what I have done was easy. It wasn't. The key to my success was opening my mind to new ideas and not letting my past disrupt my future. Some of us are dealt a shitty hand in life. It is how you play those cards that determines whether or not you win.

Understanding your Environment

In this chapter, I would like to talk about the world teenagers are living in. First, it is much different than when your parents were growing up. Do not expect them to understand exactly what you are going through because they won't. Times are changing. When they were your age, a cassette tape was a big deal. What I would like us to do is try and figure out how we can make these different generations get along with and help one another.

Twenty years ago, the family was not under as much stress to survive. If a household had two parents in it, one or both parents had to work to survive. In more fortunate situations, one parent was able to stay at home and care for the children. Today, this is not the case. It has become more expensive to live and both parents must work to make ends meet. This is not your parents' fault. If you feel as if you are second behind work, you are not. Working is a part of life. Nothing is just given to anyone. Everything must be earned or paid for. This is one concept that will not change as you become older. Thinking briefly of what you may want to do to make money is a good idea. Working is not as bad as you think it is.

I know when I was younger, the last thing I wanted to do was work. I thought having a job would take away from the time I had to hang out with friends or interfere with doing drugs. I figured I could just sell some drugs and have money without working. I am very aware that I am not the only one who thought like this. Besides, it seemed to make sense. Why would anyone want to spend time after school making six dollars an hour when you could make a hundred dollars an hour selling drugs? Yes, I am not going to lie, selling drugs is easy money.

Here is the difference between the person who makes six dollars an hour, we will call him Vic, and the person who makes a hundred dollars an hour, whom we will call Pete. Vic spends his eight-hour shift talking to customers, making sales, taking inventory, stocking shelves, counting money, making change, and sometimes dealing with complaints. Boring stuff, right? Pete hits the streets or makes some phone calls to set up a deal. One or two hours later, he is back hanging out, a hundred dollars richer. Cool. It would have taken Vic all week to make that kind of cash. By the end of the week, Vic is tired; he collects his paycheck for $120. Pete has pulled in $650. Vic puts a hundred dollars in a savings account and keeps twenty in his pocket to take his girl to see a movie. Pete goes and spends his money as quickly as he made it. He gets the coolest sneakers, buys a new stereo, and picks up a nice new chain to show off with. This goes on for some time the same way. Pete is now getting more and more customers. It seems as if he doesn't have as much time to hang with his friends as before. He drops out of school stating, "Fuck school, I am making more money than any of these other punks working."

Vic has saved enough money by now to by a used car. His girlfriend loves it and they cruise around after school and on weekends hanging out with their friends. Pete bought a brand new car and it is easier now for him to get more drugs. He gets some new hammers and puts a booming system in it. He is big time now. He has no problem getting girls because he has money to spend on them. All this quick money and a new car have brought a lot of heat on to Pete. The cops in the town are thinking, "Hey, something's strange with that Pete kid; he has all this nice stuff but doesn't work.' While Pete is driving home, the police decide to pull him over because he is speeding. Since Pete knows that for the past year, he has been selling drugs, he has no idea what the police want. He doesn't think they are going to give him a simple speeding ticket, but they are after him for selling drugs. Pete decides he does not want to find out and takes off down the road. He makes it about three miles running red lights until finally he hits a car head-on. The car Pete hits has a child in it who breaks both of his legs really badly. Pete's brand new car is destroyed.

After the police arrest Pete, they decide to do some investigating and search his house. They find drugs and add them to his charges. At this point, Vic has saved enough money to put some rims on his car and he is saving some money for a system, too. Pete is given eight years in prison for all of his crimes. No one really cares to help Pete because he doesn't have many real friends left. The people he knew liked him because he had drugs, money, and a nice car. Pete now has nothing but a small cell, an orange jumpsuit with a number on it, and some blue slippers to cover his feet. It will be eight years before Pete can touch a girl, wear normal clothes, decide when he wants to go bed, or what he wants to eat that day. He will remain in the same place unable to do anything he wants to do.

Vic now has been made a manager of the store. He graduated from high school and has learned how to make money honestly. He also was pulled over a few times but just paid the fines and moved on. Vic has a new car now and a few new girlfriends. Pete has spent his days fighting over food and trying to stay alive in the joint. You may say to yourself, "Yeah, I am not going to get caught doing crime so I do not have to worry." That was what I thought, Pete thought, and everyone sitting in prison today thought. No one in their right mind says, "I am going to sell drugs or commit crimes until I get caught and go to prison." It is strange then how America has more people in prison than any other country in the world. I guess a lot of people were wrong.

Ask yourself one thing: Is it worth it? When Pete finally gets out of prison, he will be a man, uneducated, broke, and on parole. One mistake and he goes right back in. He has no friends left and people are afraid of him. Maybe Pete and Vic could have their own stores by now. But Pete never gave himself that chance. Don't sell yourself short. Cars, clothes, and the newest sneakers are not worth your life.

Now let's try and figure out why we think we must have all this shit anyway. Every day, the kids I work with and I listen to rap music and watch music channels on the television. It became very clear that most of your role models today believe this is the crap that makes us important. Rappers talk about owning this type of car and drinking a certain type of alcohol. Most of rap music is about smoking pot and shooting people if they get in the way of their attaining it. First of all, let's try and let reality set in for a second. I know I do not need to waste much time explaining this so I will make it brief. If you shoot somebody, you will not get a car, girls, or be the most popular guy in town. You will end up a lot worse off than Pete. You will be sent to hell on earth where you will get no respect and no one will think you are the shit for doing it. I understand that we are not all going to get along, but using a gun to solve your problems is weak and flat-out stupid. I can guarantee you that no rap artist has made it to where they are by running around shooting people. They are there because they acted more like Vic than Pete. They worked hard and spent a lot of time broke and practicing in a music studio before they ever became rich. They do know if they appeal to a confused teenager's mind and tell them that being gangster and hurting people is cool, kids will listen and continue to buy their albums. Basically, all they are doing is playing you for a fool. If you live a criminal's life, you will be nothing more than a criminal. These rappers who claim to live this way do not. They are lying. If this were true, the Hip-Hop Music awards would be held in Cell Block 6. Don't get me wrong, I enjoy all types of music. I am just getting sick and tired of seeing kids I care about, just like you, letting rap music influence them into getting into trouble and locked away. Music is meant to entertain you, not be a way of life. This world is too complex to be explained in a five-minute song.

Right now, I want you take a moment and think about the five most important things in your life. Look at the list and see if these are things you already have, are close to getting, or are dreams for the future. In my list, I would already have two, am close to getting three, and four and five are dreams of mine. I feel a good list of what is important to you should look this way. Think back and try and find two things that you have done that make you proud. Remember that no one can take these two from you; they are done, in the books. Then look at something coming up that you are trying to accomplish. You may feel now the same way you did before you completed those first two goals, unsure of yourself, scared, or thinking it cannot be done. This is normal; every human being feels this way, and we are all in the same boat. You achieved these goals in the past and nothing is different now. This cycle will continue throughout your life. It will begin by you realizing what it is you want. Next, you will need to ask, how the hell can I get it? Then put your thoughts and plans into action. If at first it does not work, keep trying. Soon, number three on your list will be yours. The key is using what worked in the past to help you get number four and five done. Then make six and seven and so on. Having concrete goals for the future will give your life direction.

I found that it is hard for me to look into my past. Like me, you may be thinking, I can't think of anything good in my life. That is okay, and maybe you don't have anything good there or are unable to see it. Look at it this way, the fact you are able to even read this book shows you are smart, curious, and maybe ready to start making some changes. Your past can do one of two things, fuck up your whole future or make you stronger than ever. Let me explain using some of what I have been through…

Let's say my father decided the day he was hurt not to take his daily bike ride. He was never hit and I was born into the perfect little world. My brother and I would have probably had all the nicest toys, gone to the best private schools, and gotten the cars of our dreams when we turned sixteen. We would not have had a care in the world. I may have gone to an expensive college and majored in business like my dad. My brother may have learned how to run the auto body shop someday. We would have never had to worry about selling drugs and getting into trouble. Living this way is not all it is cracked up to be. Having everything handed to you makes you unprepared for the real world. Remember, I said no one just gives you anything. This is also true for the more fortunate. Most things they have are bought. One thing that no one can buy is life experience. That is achieved by living life.

If I grew up in this perfect environment, I would have missed out on many of the experiences that made me who I am today. If I were to bump into the Jay who had it all, I think I would not become friends with him. We just wouldn't understand one another. I can say that this other Jay may have had a difficult time dealing with problems that may occur in his life. By him not having to deal with most problems makes him weak to them. This type of person should have more to fear than you. He may run into a problem that is just too much to handle and go off the deep end. His past may have been easy but not what is needed to survive today. If we all look at our past in this way, I wouldn't give mine up for anything. You may not have had everything go your way, but you have gained experience and the ability to pick yourself up when you are down. Equipped with the knowledge of how to do this, nothing can stop you. You are tough. Use your past to your advantage. If you look back and feel you have done nothing right, you will always be haunted by it. It will follow you around like a bad dream. Be proud of your history, no matter what mistakes you have made. Today is the beginning.

I want to make this next point clear: life is hard. Every move we make will affect the next. This is not something to be afraid of, only to be aware of. The easiest way to make the right choice when we are confused is to ask somebody who knows. The best advice comes from the people you may not think are so cool: Adults. I know you're thinking, "Adults, what the fuck do they know?" The truth is, they know a lot. They have made many more decisions than you have. They have had more life experiences than we have. Choosing what you talk to adults about is important. Asking your mom, dad, or teacher whom they like better, Britney Spears or Christina Aguilera, may not be the best question. When it comes to dealing with a feeling you may have about what you are interested in or helping you deal with a problem a brother, sister, or friend may be having, these guys are your best medicine. Most likely, they have been there or know somebody who has. As much as you think adults are trying to screw you over, the truth is that most of them care. They are not supposed to be your friends. I am sure you have enough of them already. Besides, who wants a forty-year-old hanging out with you anyway? You are not just born forty. You have to be a teenager before you get there. This makes them just like us. I myself have no clue what it feels like to be a father. I can say, I think it will not be easy. I am not trying to scare you, but some day, yes, you too will be an adult...AHHH! You will try and help your kids who will think you don't know shit about life either. In your mind, you'll think, "What the hell is wrong with kids today? They are all doomed." Nothing is going to change.

Every generation is going to think the next one will fail. Life will go on and so will the world. Listening to adults may turn out to be not so bad. You may just learn something if you stop and listen. My greatest knowledge comes from those who were older than I was. My friend Tim was three years older and wiser than I. I listened and learned. I know a lot of kids don't want to hear shit anyone tries to tell them, but you've got to think for a second. It takes energy to talk; nobody just says something because they like to hear themselves speak. They are saying it because they are trying to help you. They may have been there and know what works. Sometimes, the easiest solution to your problem may be sitting right next to you. If you begin to start to trust adults, I feel things may begin to get a little easier for you.

I want to finish this chapter by saying, try and question your own environment. Look at things from a few different angles. Do not believe what you have heard just because you heard it. Listen to what someone is saying and look at it from both sides. Try and feel what others are feeling around you. Take advice as much as possible and look people in the eyes when you are talking, let them know you're no fool; you know what's up.

Peer Pressure

This will be one of the most important topics discussed in this book. Peer pressure is a silent enemy that can strike without warning. You may not figure out that you are being tricked until it is too late. I will try and help you to identify what peer pressure is and some ways to remove yourself from a bad situation. First, let's begin by looking for some reasons a person would waste their time putting pressure on you to do something.

1. This person or group of people is trying to make a fool out of you. You have suddenly become their form of cruel entertainment. The problem with this is you will not be laughing, just they. You will not know this until you have already done what they have asked you to do; at this point, it is too late. Here are a couple of examples: You are in class and your so-called friends tell you to take a piece of balled-up paper and throw it at the teacher. You do it and everybody laughs. You may get a laugh as well, but end up in the principal's office in trouble, even suspended from school. While you are grounded for weeks, your friends are still in school. They are not sitting around saying, "Man that kid is cool, he is crazy, man; he threw a piece of paper at the teacher." They are probably saying, "What an idiot that kid is; he will do anything for attention." You will not know this because when you return to school they will all act like your friends

and tell you, "Dude, that was awesome when you threw that paper at the teacher; man, she was pissed." You will feel good about what you have done and begin to feel as if it was worth all the trouble you have gone through. It's not. They are telling you this so they can get you to do something stupid again. The only person, who looks cool in the eyes of these kinds of people, is the kid who has the ability to trick you into doing something that is going to hurt yourself. Don't be a fool...you have your own brain, use it.

2.   A person may also want to put peer pressure on you because no one likes to get in trouble alone. It is much more fun to a troublemaker if he has someone else to get in trouble with. I bet you can all think of the friend who always has the idea, you know, that great plan about something that always ends up with you and he in trouble. Isn't it funny how you both end up in trouble every time? Here is an example. Your "friend" says to you..."Hey, let's go into that store over there and get that new video game we want. You act as look-out while I grab it." You think to yourself, I am not stealing the game so what do I care? Your friend is thinking, "If I get caught, so are they and I am not the only stupid person doing this." They will not ask you to be a lookout outside of the store...right? They will want you to be close enough to them so you are directly involved. The reason for this is if something goes down, you are both involved. Your friend is able to justify his actions this way. He will have someone to share his criminal side with and feel that he is not so bad because he is not the only one who wants to steal.

What I am about to say next is very important...DO NOT ALLOW OTHER PEOPLE TO BRING YOU DOWN WITH THEM!!!!!!! I see this happening every day at my work...Kids drag other kids into their problems this way. You may be a good person but your friends suck. They suck so bad they suck you right down with them. You know what I am talking about. This is the guy or girl that deep down you are afraid to hang out with because you know all they want to do is get both of you in trouble. Let's face it, you are afraid of this person but do not know how to stop hanging around with them. Here is an easy solution: Stop hanging around with this person. He or she does not give a shit about you. They will not be there for you when you need them.

Let's go back to the store and I will show you. You are looking out for your friend stealing the game. All of a sudden he says, "Grab it; I will look out for you." Feeling pressured, you forget where your friend is and you steal the video game. Next thing you know, the camera above has spotted you and a security guard grabs your jacket. You look around for your "friend" whom you were backing up before. Hmmm, he is nowhere to be found. He is smart enough to know not to stand too close to you while you took the game. He knows this because he is thinking like a criminal. You didn't put any pressure on him, he put it on you. Result, you are arrested and he is home playing his old video games. There is nothing positive about this relationship. You and this person's only connection is that he or she has the ability to control you. If you stop hanging out with them, they will think they have lost that ability and move on to someone they can control. This is fine just as long as that person is not you. Trust me, they will not miss you one bit. You will not miss them either.

3. Have you ever taken the fall for someone? Sure, we all have. Why? Peer pressure. Again, you are around a person who has the ability to control you. I mean, we must not be thinking too clearly to get in trouble for something we didn't even do, but this happens all the time. We need to realize right away that whoever is asking you to take their blame is not your friend. Real friends help each other, not try to hurt each other. If you agree to take the blame for this person, it will happen over and over again. You will become the kid who doesn't care to take the fall. If you stop and think about this for a second... it sounds crazy, right? Why the hell are you going to get in trouble for something you didn't even do? You're not, because you're never going to do this again, okay? I know when someone is asking you to take the blame, they may sound very convincing. Something like this, "Oh shit, man! Dude, if I get caught for this again, I am fucked.

Just say you did it; you have never been in trouble for this, come on, man we're boys." Again I will say...you're not boys, your true boys or girls would not ask this of you. Second, the reason you have not ever been in trouble for this is because you are smart enough to not get in trouble for this shit. Third, you need to tell this person NO!! Trust me, if this kid keeps acting this way, he or she won't be around very long anyway. They will be locked up somewhere. Stand your ground and do not be taken advantage of.

4.   Drugs! When a lot of us think of peer pressure we think of being pressured into doing drugs. This is definitely true. Peer pressure and drugs go perfectly together. Let's figure out why. We all know drugs are not good for anyone. They can quickly change who we are, what we care about, what friends we choose to hang around with, and what kind of future we have. People who use drugs do not like to do them alone. It goes back to my second example; people do not feel so bad about themselves if they are not the only one doing it. The reason drugs are good to pressure you with is because you are always going to naturally be tempted to try them. You are curious to see what all the hype is about. Let me tell you, you're not missing out on anything. All a guy or girl has to do is give you that extra little push. They know this because it has been going on for hundreds of years this way. It is effective. This is the same way every person has tried drugs. I can't think of anyone I know, including myself, who decided to just go down the street, buy some weed, and smoke a blunt by myself for the first time. It just doesn't happen. Most likely, you will or have been at a party and people are smoking it and ask you if you want some. You don't want to look as if you are not down, so feeling pressured, you smoke it. Fine, don't worry, you're not the first one. This is how it happens to us all.

This also happens a lot with cigarettes. At first, you only smoke weed or cigarettes when you are around other people doing them. You feel part of the crowd. Next, you will buy your own pack or get your own joint and smoke with friends. Eventually, you will need to smoke alone to fill this need. You are no different than the rest of us in this way. These things are masters at taking over the body. You will now try and find other kids you can pressure into doing drugs or smoking so you do not feel alone. The cycle continues. We need to try and break that cycle. You are not born needing a cigarette or a joint, but somehow, there you are smoking a pack a day and getting high all the time. Why? It was a slow process but we all end up the same: Addicted. Now you are throwing away five dollars a day to kill yourself. Not cool. You have enough to worry about without intentionally doing harm to your body. Remember when you were good at sports? Now you cannot even run down the street or get away from the police...just kidding.

You see, I used pot as an example but the same applies for all drugs and alcohol. You will eventually be in a situation where people are using harder drugs. You will feel the pressure and, if you break, the more drugs you will try and the more problems you will have. Let me put it this way... When you are watching the MTV Music Awards, or movie awards, have you ever heard a rapper, singer, or movie star who has won an award say during their speech, "Well, I have to thank cocaine, marijuana, cigarettes, vodka, and crack for this award. Before I started using these drugs, I was a loser, but now that I am all fucked up, my career has taken off." No, of course not. They would never have gotten to where they are using all those drugs. I know what I am asking you to do is easier said than done. You will most likely be asked to drink or do drugs a lot in your lifetime. It is a sad fact. But what is good to know, I, and probably you also, have never seen anyone hold a person down and force them to do drugs. In the end, you have the control to make that decision. Do yourself a favor, make the right choice. Your life depends on it.

5. Sex is another serious concern for peer pressure. We will cover this topic later in the book. It is so important I am devoting an entire chapter to this.

Now that we have identified some specific examples of peer pressure, let's try and see how we can avoid all peer pressure situations. I have a very simple solution, but I am going to need you to work with me on this concept.

How often do you have small conversations with yourself throughout the day? What I mean is when you have an idea, it almost always seems as if you discuss it with yourself before you actually do it. One side of your brain looks at the negative and one side looks at the positive. Let me give you an example because I am starting to confuse myself on this. Your friends have asked you to skip school tomorrow and go to the mall with them. That night, while you are lying in bed, you begin to think about tomorrow and what to do. As you think, you begin to talk to yourself inside your head. This is normal; we all do it. This is your body's way of making decisions. The reason you are putting so much thought into it is because you know that what you are going to maybe do tomorrow is wrong and not good for you. Your brain is trying to tell itself to make the right decision. You may then tell yourself, "Man, I got to do it. My friends will think I am pussy if I don't." Then you say, "Shit, if I get caught, I may get suspended and grounded." This mental fight could go on all night until morning. One side of your brain is right. Your conscience is trying to tell you not to hurt yourself. It is the same way you would pull your hand away from a hot stove. Your body knows how to avoid pain. This is the same in decision making. We know the difference between right and wrong, but sometimes, we choose wrong.

Okay, let's assume you did decide to skip school and go to the mall. You get caught. You are not surprised because last night while you lay in bed, you knew getting caught was possible. You get suspended and grounded as predicted. Your friends are now nowhere to be found. They are dealing with their own consequences while you begin to have more mental conversations. Your brain starts to yell at you. You think to yourself: "What an idiot I am. I knew I was going to get caught, now I am in a shitload of trouble." That voice you are hearing is the same voice you should have listened to in the first place. Now you have to listen to your conscience tell you it was right. It is almost laughing at you. It will be laughing at you every time something comes up you want to do for the next month you are grounded.

This voice will always be there. It will come out throughout your life every time you need to make a decision. The voice will always be right. Let's look at it from the other side. You make the right decision and go to school. Your friends all get caught. Immediately, the voice will come out to congratulate you. It will say, "Psew, I am glad I didn't do that." You will immediately feel good about yourself. Even if your friends call you and make fun of you for not going, you will know deep down that you made the right choice and that is really all that matters. You must do what is in your own best interests. When it really comes down to it, you are all you got. You have to answer to yourself.

Your own voice will always know the best choice you should make in any situation. It has the ability to make you feel uncomfortable about something. This is good. It is your body's way of telling you to get out of the situation or make a smart decision before you get hurt. When you begin to hear the voice, you should stop and listen because it is trying to help you. Let's think about this. You do not sit up all night thinking about the shower you are going to take in the morning, right? The reason is, the shower is not going to cause you any harm. You will sit up thinking about important decisions you need to make that affect your future. In any peer pressure situation, your voice will be there yelling at you. Listen to it. It is your best friend. You will have to answer to this voice for the rest of your life. Don't piss it off; you're only hurting yourself.

I listen to my voice in every action I make. It is not easy to do, but I have built up years of trust with my voice. When I have not listened, I have ended up in trouble. I learned from my mistakes. I was getting tired of hearing it laugh at me after I made the wrong choice. For the most part, my voice tells me that what I am doing is right and thinking things through is good for me. Of course, no one is perfect. We are all going to make wrong choices and be fooled by peer pressure and others in our lives. It is important to try and not continue to make the same mistakes over and over again. Let me give you a quick little example of this that always makes me laugh when I hear it at work, and I do hear this at least three times a year from completely different kids I work with.

A lot of the boys I work with have been placed on parole and committed for eighteen months to the state on drug charges. A majority of them have been caught selling drugs. I don't mean they were Al Pacino in *Scarface*, selling pounds of weed or kilos of cocaine. These guys were selling enough to get a small amount of cash without having to work for it. Throughout the year they are with me, I will try my best to tell these individuals that you will always get caught and end up in jail with nothing. I have seen it over and over again. They love to look at me and say, "I know, Jay, I am not going to sell drugs when I get out. I am going to go to school and get a job." This is what they tell me. I am their staff. They may only tell me what I want to hear. What is sometimes really going on, when I am not around, is they are telling the other boys, "When I get out, I am not going to sell on that street corner I got caught on before. It is too hot!" or, "I just need to stay away from that cop; he is on to me now." His so-called friends are saying, "Yeah, you're right, bro, you just got played last time."

This will go on throughout the boy's stay at my facility. He will be telling the staff one thing but thinking another. After about fourteen months with me, he gets out and begins his master plan. The other boys will now begin to tell me about what his real motives are. I will always ask, "Is he planning to sell drugs?" Eighty percent of the time they say, "Yes, but he is doing it smart now." This comment always makes me laugh. Usually, it works for about two months and he is caught again for selling drugs. Since he is now over juvenile criminal age, he has serious adult drug charges. There is no smart way to sell drugs or commit any criminal act. The only smart way to avoid getting caught for a crime is, DO NOT COMMIT ANY CRIMES. This is the foolproof way to avoid getting arrested or getting in any trouble. It took me most of my teenage life and many lonely nights locked up somewhere to figure this out. I am telling you because I know. Do not think you are smart enough to get away with anything. These people who continue to make the same mistake over and over again are obviously not the criminal geniuses they make themselves out to be. You are no different. The sooner you realize this, the sooner you can begin to use your brain to do something positive in your life.

School

School. I cannot stress how important school is in your future. I don't mean how popular you are, what friends you have, or whom you took to the big dance. I mean how much you learned, how prepared you are for college, and what skills and talents you have that society will pay you for in the future. I would not be honest if I didn't tell you again; the only way to really make money in the future is by working for it. If you are able to inherit all the money you need for the future or win the lotto, then you might as well put down this book and start reading the *Wall Street Journal* every day. For the rest of us, working is our future. You must realize that school and work go hand in hand. What you do in the future to make money completely depends on what kind of education you have received. This is a lot of pressure. I understand this, but it is the truth. The rest of your life will be affected by how you perform now. Once you begin to work full time, it is very difficult to go back and correct mistakes you have made in your education. You will need to start immediately. It will not seem as if it pays off now, or does it? I tell the kids I work with that at this point in their life, school is their job. They always reply by saying, "If school is my job, then where is my paycheck?"

You are getting paid; you are investing in your future. If that isn't enough, I will break it down into dollar amounts to show you how much money you are making while in school.

High-School Dropout:

If you choose to drop out of high school, you can hope to find a job starting you off at minimum wage. In today's economy, even finding this job will be difficult. There are going to be many other people competing for this type of work. But let's say you got the job. Your hourly rate will be around $6.75 per hour. You will need to start working at the age of sixteen. You will be able to retire at the age of sixty-five. You will work eight hours a day, five days a week, fifty weeks a year for forty-nine years. After doing the math, I figured you will make $661,500 in your career. You are in school for six hours a day, five days a week, forty weeks a year for ten years. If you break that down into how much your schooling is worth compared to future earning potential, it equals that your hourly rate for school is $55 dollars an hour. That is more than most adults make in America.

High-School Graduate:

With a high school diploma, you will most likely get a job making $10 an hour. You will begin working at the age of eighteen. You will work forty-seven years until retirement. You will make $940,000 in your lifetime of work. You will have been in school for twelve years. Your hourly rate for school is $65 dollars an hour.

College Graduate:

With a college degree, you could find a job staring at about $18 dollars an hour. You will begin working at the age twenty-one. You will work forty-two years until retirement. You will make $1,512,000. You would have been in school for sixteen years. Your hourly rate at school would be $79 dollars an hour. That is close to what a doctor or lawyer makes.

Master's Degree:

With a master's degree, you could easily find a job making $30 dollars an hour. You will begin working at the age of twenty-three. You will work for forty years until retirement. You will make $2,400,000 in your working career. You will have been in school for eighteen years. Your hourly rate at school would be $166 dollars an hour. That is what doctors and lawyers make.

You may not see an actual paycheck at the end of a school week, but, trust me, you are getting paid. You are making as much as people in the best-paying careers in our society every day you are in school. Also, you will be working the rest of your adult life. Why would you not want to postpone that as long as possible?

Your education is very valuable and will need to be earned. Nowhere in our country are you going to make over a hundred and fifty dollars an hour at your age except in school. So right now, you are working in the best job you can. You would have to be crazy to give up your $150-an-hour job (school) to go and make $6.75. I made that mistake when I dropped out of high school. I am just glad I realized it before it was too late for me. Do not think it is too late for you.

I know a lot of kids who tell me that school is too hard for them. I will always respond by asking how much time they put into going to school or doing their homework. They usually say, "I do not put much time in at all because it is too hard for me." Well, of course it is going to be hard if you do not practice at school. Think about it like this: When you were trying to learn how to ride a bike or get good at a video game, you were not good at it until you took the time to learn and practice. School is no different. The more you put into it, the easier it becomes. I could guarantee that if you spent as much time doing your schoolwork as you do playing Grand Theft Auto, you would have straight As.

Most of us look at school in negative manner. Why is this? Why is educating ourselves and learning a bad thing? It's not as if everyone hates to learn to do new things, right? When Sony releases a new game or a new television program is going to air, we don't say, "Oh, I am not going to get that game or watch that show because I do not want to learn about it." School has just been given a bad rap over the years. Kids who do well are called geeks or nerds and kids who cut class and fail are considered cool. I felt the same way. I was always making fun of the kids who were concerned about their grades and had plans for the future. These are the same kids who probably now are making $200,000 a year and traveling all over the world. I guess they do not feel like nerds anymore. I would have to say these kids were not nerds at all. They just knew the importance of getting a good education for their future. I know you may disagree with what I am saying surrounding school, but it is the truth.

I am going to let you in on a little secret about the society we live in. America cannot function without uneducated people in it. We need high school dropouts and lots of them. Who else is going to pump our gas, serve us our fast-food meals, wash our cars, bag our groceries, rent us our movies, or clean up our bathrooms? If everybody had a masters degree's there would be some pretty well-educated janitors running around. Look at it this way, how many of the people you know say, "When I grow up, I want to work at McDonald's." I can't think of anyone I know, can you? No, of course not, but somehow there is a McDonalds in every other town in America. Wow, that is strange. How can all these McDonalds have so many employees if nobody wants to work there? They can because most of their employees made the mistake of leaving their $150-dollar-an-hour school job to take an eight-dollar-an-hour job cooking hamburgers. Our society depends on these people. No one is going to feel bad for them because we all want our burgers our way. We need these people. Don't get me wrong, if you are just starting to work, these are great jobs to have after school to make some money, but choosing a career as a sandwich artist just isn't going to pay the bills. Besides, don't you know you are better than that?

Another issue kids tell me they do not like about school has to do with their teachers. My kids say, "I don't mind school; I just hate my teachers." Let's try and look at what's going on here with these damn teachers. I can bet that before you start each school year, your friends give their rundown on your upcoming teachers. I am sure you hear things like this: "Oh, that Mrs. Wilson. You're going to hate her. She is a fucking bitch," or: "Mr. Davidson, he sucks. You're going to hate his class." Most of the time, you hear how much the teacher sucks but you never really know why. Probably the reason this person hates the teacher is because that teacher tried to help that student learn. Since we think school sucks, if a teacher tries to make us learn something we hate, they must suck, too. The teachers that a lot of kids tend to like are those teachers who do not care whether we learn or not. They just teach and let the student make his or her own choices.

During school, you will come across both types of teachers. The ones you or your friends think suck should be the ones you are taking advantage of. These teachers who want to help you are perfect tools who can be used to build up your grades. This will only come if both people are willing to help each other. A teacher is not going to continue to help you if you do not try and accept the help. If you keep fighting a teacher's help, they will eventually give up and spend their energy on a student who wants to be helped. This is understandable. Why should they be wasting all that valuable time when others need help, too? If you were to accept the help given, the teacher would spend the entire year making sure you learned and achieved. With the right teacher and your cooperation, you may surprise yourself on how quickly you begin to like school and learning.

School can be like a drug in its own way. Once you accept that you are student, and you must learn whether or not you like it, you may find that you get addicted to it. As you begin to find subjects that interest you, they become exciting to learn about. The more you begin to learn about something, the more you are able to apply what you already know to what you are learning. The learning then becomes easier. Once learning becomes easy and fun, what else can we complain about? I mean really, let's think about what we have learned already. You are making $150 dollars an hour to do something you like. Man, I wish I were in your shoes.

As we all get older, you will start to hear your friends begin to talk about things they wish they had done differently when they were younger. The number one thing I hear my friends say is: "I wish I worked harder in school. If I could go back now, I would go to every class and do all my homework." This is true for most adults who didn't take school seriously. The reason for this is, once you get older and are trying to pay your bills to pay rent, afford a new car, or take the vacation you have been dreaming of, you realize how important having the money to do all these things is. They then look back and say, "Shit, I spent all that time sitting in school just fucking around. I should have been working on graduating. If I did, I could have all these things now." Let me try and explain a little more why most people regret things they did in the past when, at the time, they knew they should have made better choices. I know it is hard to think about the future. It is the same reason you may think, hey, what is this guy talking about? I am not making $150 dollars an hour at school. I see no money now. We all only think about the upcoming week. We are remembering yesterday and worrying about tomorrow. If doing well in school doesn't fit into tomorrow's plans, screw it, right? When you become an adult, nothing changes. We are still remembering yesterday and worrying about tomorrow. Your problems are just different. Adults realize that if they worked harder in the past, life would be easier now. You are in school for twelve years; you will be working for forty-five. If working hard for twelve makes the other forty-five easier, that is a great deal. Or you spend the next forty-five years kicking yourself in the ass wondering why you didn't work hard for only twelve years in school. Are you going to spend 10,000 dollars on a car that's worth only 1,000? No, you would be a sucker. Well, dropping your education is like dropping $10,000 on that piece-of-shit car. Don't let this deal pass you by.

Let me also clear up a myth about college. A lot of people claim that you need to be rich to go to college. Not true. Anyone can attend college if they are accepted. There are billions of dollars in scholarship money just waiting to be given out. Just as society needs the uneducated, we also need the well-educated. This is the category I would like everyone who reads my book to fall under. Scholarship money can be given to any student who has been accepted into college. Your grades and S.A.T. scores will determine if you are accepted into college, not how much money you have in your bank account. Once accepted, you can receive free money. All students whose parents cannot afford to send their kids to college are eligible and will receive financial aid. This money will need to be paid back. The catch is you will be able to get a good job when you are done to pay it back. It is nice how that works. Oh, you have thirty years to pay it back. If there is one thing about your future I do not want you to worry about, it is paying back your student loans. You will cross that bridge when you get there.

We need to focus on getting you into college. SATs are important but are not everything. Make sure you take them and take them a few times so you get practice. They only keep your best score. Apply to as many schools as you can. Once accepted, even if it is not the school of your choice, go. You can always transfer in the future to that school, when you have proved your grades are good in college. I went to school with very little help from anyone but from the school I attended. I am paying my loans back now, but they are small payments stretched over thirty years; don't sweat it. Shit, I am going back to school as we speak. THERE IS NO SUCH THING AS HAVING TOO MUCH EDUCATION!!!

I would like to change gears and talk about some of school's educational value that may not be so obvious. School is basically the first place you will begin to learn how to be social. What I mean by this is you will start to learn how to interact with others and get a feeling for how people like to be treated. Learning these skills is as important as getting an education. I could not get any job with any amount of education if I did not know how to talk to people. If I were to go for a job interview and I told the boss, "Yo, I am here for that crap job you have posted," I would not make it through the first interview question.

In society, how you conduct yourself with others is very important for what opportunities will open for you. A person will form their impression of you within the first thirty seconds of meeting you. They will know whether or not they like you. Being polite and honest with people is most important in getting what you want. Having others gain trust in you is easy, if you know how to handle yourself. You do not want people to think you don't care about them or they will not care about you. When you are at school, you are learning to become the kind of person you will be in the future. If you treat everybody like assholes at school, you will most likely treat people like shit for the rest of your life. In turn, you will be treated like shit for the rest of your life. I am not asking you to change who you are or what you believe in. I am asking you to start and consider how people at your school think of you and how you treat others in school. Maybe how you think others view you is not altogether true. I know a lot of the kids I deal with who act up in school think they are cool. The other boys all laugh when they are swearing at a teacher. They tell the kid, "Holy shit, you're crazy." But when I talk to those same kids about poor behavior displayed at school, they tell me, "That kid is fucking stupid. All the teacher was trying to do was help him." Look at how you act in school and maybe your opinion of the way you treat others will change.

I could sit here and talk about school with you for the rest of this book, but that would get very boring. I have made a few very valuable points in this chapter. Most importantly, remember, you are still young. You have one shot at your education. Make the most of it and I promise you it will pay you back more than you could ever imagine.

Understanding Sexual Encounters

There is a lot to consider when it comes to sexual encounters at a young age or any age. This will be a difficult chapter for us to understand together. But at this point, I hope I have gained your trust. I want you to think back at how many times I hit on a subject that you were familiar with. I want you to understand that I know what you are feeling. Remember that I, too, was a teenager not too long ago.

I have been working with sexually active boys for five years now. Believe me when I say I have heard it all when it comes to how they look at sex and how they feel about those involved in sex. It is not pretty. This chapter may be hard to listen to, but it is the truth.

We will begin by laying out several questions you must ask yourself before becoming sexually active.

1. Are you responsible enough to handle sexual pressure from others once becoming sexually active?

2. Are you aware of methods of contraception and items that protect you from sexually transmitted diseases or unwanted pregnancies?

3. What influences are making you consider sexual activity?

4. Are you in love?

5. Is peer pressure a factor?

6. Are you making the best decision for your future?

Let's examine each one of these questions in more detail.

1. *Are you responsible enough to handle sexual pressure from others once becoming sexually active?* This is very important to consider. You kids today have it rough. Sex is everywhere you turn. I understand why you feel the need to be part of a sex-crazed society. What needs to be understood is that sex comes with a lot a sacrifice and pain for those involved. Sexual responsibility is much more difficult than you may think. Losing your innocence can affect the rest of your life and how you are perceived by others around you. Let me explain to you how I see sexual pressure in teenage life today. Once you turn about twelve years old, your body begins to experience changes. You start to develop hair in areas you once had none. Breast size increases in girls, and boys and girls begin to become more attracted to one another. These are the basics of puberty. Your body is becoming ready to be sexually active. This is natural; we have all experienced these changes. You may be further along in your development right now, but as in all humans, it begins with puberty.

Your friends will begin to say things like: "That boy is cute," or "Man, she is really hot." You will start to really take pride in your appearance. Fashion and looking attractive becomes number one in your life. This is fun; a whole new world is beginning to open up for you. In this new sexual world, there are many dangers and problems that result from sex. Learning them now and understanding the risks is very important in protecting yourself from others. You need to begin by recognizing that others around you are going through these same changes. You all will begin to become more curious about sexual activity and exploring your attractions to others. This is very natural and must start off slowly. Flirting and kissing other boys and girls is where it should end until you are an adult. You are not responsible enough in your teens to handle all the pressure and consequences that come with becoming sexually active at a young age. Keep your innocence and protect your dignity. If you are sexually active at this point, stop immediately and take a step back. It is not too late to build back up your pride and respect you should have for yourself. Do not let others use your body to explore their natural curiosities surrounding sex.

2.   *Are you aware of methods of contraception and items that protect you from sexually transmitted diseases or unwanted pregnancies?* I understand that, regardless of what I say about staying away from sex until you are an adult, kids are having a lot of sex at a young age. Protecting yourself during these engagements is the least you can do for yourself and others. The trouble in our country is we do not want to admit that our youth are involved in these activities. We would rather not try and protect our kids. Instead, we hope the problem will just go away. You will not know if the person you are engaging in sexual activity with has diseases or not. This person is considered to be too young by our standards to be tested for STDs (Sexually Transmitted Diseases). Most likely, if they are engaging in such activities at a young age, you are not the only person they are, or have been, with sexually. This means that when you are having unprotected sex with that person, you are actually having unprotected sex with anyone else he or she has had unprotected sex with. Got it? It is a scary thought but true. You will not be able to look at a person and tell how many people they have had unprotected sex with. They will not have a sign on their head saying "I have a disease." They may not even know themselves. This is a risk you do not want to take.

Many STDs are incurable. You will now have to spend the rest of your life walking around with a disease. How are you going to feel when you meet the person you may want to spend the rest of your life with and have to tell him or her that you have an STD? That person is not going to feel the same way you do anymore. Using a condom is an excellent way to help prevent an STD or pregnancy. (I am not going to get into too much detail surrounding pregnancy until later in the chapter.) The problem with condoms is they break or fall off during sex. You may think you are protecting yourself, but in reality, you are still at risk. The best way to keep safe is to avoid sexual contact or stay with one sexual partner only. Do not be embarrassed for you and your partner to go get tested for STDs before taking your relationship to a sexual level. This would be admired by adults and shows you are aware of the dangers surrounding sex.

3. *What influences are making you consider sexual activity?* Let me think.... T.V? Or M.T.V., B.E.T. or maybe V.H.1? Magazines? Movies? Yes, these channels. Books and movies, as much as kids love to watch and read them, do not have your best sexual interests in mind. They actually are very aware of your sexual curiosities and play right into this. They flash sexual images, half-naked singers, and have spring-break bikini contests because they know you watch this stuff. In turn, you will begin to think that everyone is having sex at a young age so why should you be any different? The reason is, what you see on television is much different than what actually goes on in real life. Television is all about the commercials. Without the commercials, channels could not stay on the air. The advertisers pay a lot of money to have their commercials played on the hottest channels. They want you to watch what the singers and rappers are doing because you then go out and buy the latest style that they are wearing. It all comes back to money. If Britney Spears is wearing a short tight sexy miniskirt from Guess, you think to yourself, I got to have that new skirt. If 50 Cent is wearing a new style of hat, you want the hat. Having the hottest gear comes from advertisers working off your sexual curiosities. You want to be noticed by others around you at school. You and everyone else your age use clothes to do that. Clothes make you stand out in a crowd. You can determine how you want to be perceived by others around you by what you wear. This is very important for you at this point in your life. Wearing an outfit that is too revealing sends a signal

to others that you want them to look at your body and have sexual thoughts about you. This is not a smart move. Boys are not looking at you thinking how nice you look in that mini skirt. Instead, they are saying how they want to hit that ass. That is it. They could care less who you are or about building a relationship with you. If you do not control your sexual activity, boys and/or girls will look at you as a slut, or a person who sleeps with people to get attention. Meanwhile, the attention you will be getting is not the kind you had in mind. Boys and girls will spend their free time talking about each other's sexual behaviors. Save yourself the aggravation. When your name comes up, don't give them shit to talk about. Keep your name out of the mud; you'll be happy you did down the road.

4. *Are you in love?* When I was a teenager, I always thought I was in love with my current girlfriend. After about a month of dating, I would make the big step and tell them I loved them. At the time, I actually did think I was in love with this girl. Then, after a few months, I would see a new girl I liked and dump the old one for her. This cycle continued the same way for many of my teenage years. I wasn't actually in love with any of these girls. I just had no clue what love was all about. You have not had the time yet in your life to be truly in love with your boyfriend or girlfriend. Of course, you will have feelings for people that go beyond friendship. This is good. These feelings can be somewhat dangerous. These feelings are the beginning of what makes this relationship different from your other friendships. These types of relationships can be the best times in your life and the worst. I am sure, like me, you have had your heart broken by someone already. This is common; your feelings for a person may be stronger than theirs for you. Usually, in every relationship, someone walks away hurt. You need to take your relationships slowly. Do not become too close to people too quickly. If you do not take your time, you may find that you are getting your heart broken all the time. This is happening because the other person in the relationship is taking their time. They are going slowly and trying to figure out how much

time they want to spend with you. If they feel you are getting too involved too quickly, they may become scared and move on without you.

One of the best ways you can control the pace of a relationship is with sex. Do not let the other person determine how fast the sexual side of your relationship is going to go. Remember that it is your body and only you will say who can do what to it when. Besides, the person in this relationship may only be talking with you because he or she wants sex from you. If you do not give the relationship time to develop without sex, you may find these people still leaving you, and they got want they wanted by using you. Take your time; you have a lot of it left.

5. *Is peer pressure a factor?* Pressure is always a factor when it comes to sex. First, your partner may be putting pressure on you by trying to make you feel that if you do not have sex with them, they will leave you. If this is the case, this person does not have true feelings for you. If they did, they would not be trying to get you to do something you are not ready to do. They are not the nice person you think they are. They are in this relationship for different reasons than you are. End this relationship and do not feel badly about it. You made the right decision and kept control of your body.

How many times have you heard your friends ask questions like: "Man, did you hit it yet?" or: "What did you guys do last night?" They want to know the answers to these questions because they want to try and decide what they should do in their own relationship by looking at what you are doing in yours. Your behavior will determine what your friends are doing and vice versa. If you are having sex with your boyfriend or girlfriend, it won't be too long before your friends are having sex with theirs. This is peer pressure at its finest. Nobody wants to feel left out, so they are going to engage in the same activities you are, even if these activities are not in anyone's best interest right now. If friends are choosing to have sexual relationships, it does not mean you need to be. If your friends said they were going to run out into oncoming traffic after school, I would hope you would have the sense not to join them. Sex is very risky business and should be taken seriously at all times. Instead of joining in their poor judgment, try and help them make better decisions in the future. You will see that they will look up to you for advice because you are stronger than the average person who just does what everyone else is doing because they do not have the sense to make their own choices.

6. *Are you making the best decision for your future?* As talked about earlier in the chapter, sex comes with a price. The ultimate price is bringing a child into the world whom you are not mature enough to raise, are not financially secure enough to support, or who does not have a mother or father to be there for them. Increasingly, I see younger girls with kids of their own. The problem is they are still a kid themselves, even though their body was mature enough to have a child. It does not mean they are anywhere close to being mentally ready for the type of commitment it takes to properly raise a child. I am twenty-six years old and am still nowhere near ready to make that commitment in my life. Children need more and more support as our country becomes a harder place to grow up in. Kids need vast amounts of love and attention, as well as money, to keep them properly clothed, fed, educated, and active. Having a strong family support system is also a must. If you feel as a teenager that you can provide all these necessities, then maybe you are ready to be a mother or father. I know that the kids I was working with had a lot to learn about straightening out their own lives, let alone raising another. Kids are not something that you must have to feel like an adult. Giving yourself the chance to become an adult will give you that feeling. Kids do not go away. They will need your care for the rest of your life. Give your future the chance to make something out of you, before you choose to raise and teach a child about life.

I have one more area of concern I would like to talk about before we finish the chapter. With recent advances in technology comes more danger to younger children who are looking for sexual answers in the wrong places. Be extremely cautious with whom you talk on the Internet. This is no place to screw around. Sexual predators, rapists, and murders have found this to be an excellent tool to gain a young person's trust. Trust me when I say this, just because it sounds like the truth on the computer does not mean it is. Some people are very good at convincing you they are something they are not. Never give a stranger on the Internet any personal information about you or your family. This includes photos, addresses, phone numbers, and pretty much anything that can give this person a map to find you. It may seem like fun to talk to people on the Internet, but the results of what could happen will be far from fun. Use the Internet to talk with friends you know in person only. If someone is interested in you online, it is for all the wrong reasons.

I will finish the chapter by saying…follow your heart and let your feelings be your guide. Make sure you think about all your actions before acting.

Talking to your Parents and Adults

Okay, I know what you are thinking, adults are the enemy, right? Sometimes, but not always. When I was young, I did everything in my power to stay clear of my parents and teachers. This may not have been a wise decision. This forced me to kind of raise myself. I did not look for advice from adults and tended to make all my decisions on my own. Obviously, this was not a good idea. I was in trouble every week and eventually ended up in jail. In this chapter, I would like to show you some ways you can communicate with adults without thinking they do not understand what it is you want or need.

Here is a simple way you can ask your parents for something you want. First, do not approach your mother or father and ask, "Hey, can you get me this new pair of sneakers at the mall?" This is not a good approach to any question. It is rude, and you already sound as if you will not appreciate the fact that they are willing to help you out. In most situations, your parents will probably say no, not because they do not want to get you the sneakers, but because of the way you ask for them. Here is a better approach. Start by asking your parents if there is anything they need done around the house. Then explain how you saw some new sneakers at the mall today and would like to make some money to earn them. Usually, there is always something you can do to help your parents. You do a little work and maybe your parents say, "Okay, help clean up the yard and we will go get the sneakers." Now everyone is happy. You got the sneakers, your parents feel you are learning to be responsible, and the yard is cleaned up. Do you see how we approached this problem using our brain a bit? We came to the adult with a solution and a compromise. We said we are willing to earn this instead of sounding greedy and that we do not deserve to have everything handed to us.

Let's look at another way you can gain you parents' trust and show them you are maturing and can be trusted. This is what all parents are looking for in their children: Responsibility. I know, responsibility is a scary word, but it means everything to adults. Let's say your curfew is 10:00 on Fridays. You want to go and see a movie with friends; it does not get out until 11:00. You ask you parents very nicely, because that is the first step to get what you want. Next, if they say yes, you make sure you return by 11:00. You got to do what you wanted and you returned on time, showing you are responsible and you can handle staying out later. You are showing that you are growing up. If you were to take advantage of them cutting you a break and returned at midnight, you may get in more trouble and have your curfew knocked down to 9:00. Won't you feel like an idiot when you friends are out till 11:00, and you have to be home at 9:00? Sounds silly when all you had to do is show a little responsibility. The only person you are hurting by not following the rules is yourself. Your parents do not have to be in at 9:00 because you screwed up. YOU have to be home early. Remember that your behavior impacts you directly and others around you. Think these situations through carefully before upsetting your parents and breaking their trust.

Just being polite, using the manners that you all know, is one of the first steps to changing the way others perceive you, especially adults. Try saying the words "please" and "thank you" a few times a day. I guarantee that you will be treated with more respect and that people will begin to take you more seriously.

Charm. Using charm when you speak to adults will get you very far in this world. Adults today think most kids are heading downhill. The kids I work with have very little knowledge on how to speak to adults, teachers, police, judges, or basically anyone older than themselves. This lack of charm has not gotten them very far. They do not even give an adult a chance to understand their point of view before they start acting like an idiot. *Example:* As a kid you have rules set in place that need to be followed. If you break a rule, it is not going to be one of your friends who are going to yell at you. Most likely, it will be an adult. It is the adult's job to make sure that kids are following rules. These rules are set in place for a reason. If an adult tells you what you did was wrong and you return by calling him or her names, you are now digging yourself a deeper hole. This person is not going to be so quick to help you out. They are still the ones who are going to be in control of your punishment. It is not their fault that you chose to break the rule in the first place. If you were to use some charm and explain that you are sorry for breaking the rule and will work harder in the future, your punishment may be less severe. You treated the adult with respect and got respect in return. This is a very important skill to have in life. Treating others with respect will take you to the top. If you do not learn this skill, adults will pick up on it very quickly. You will think you are being nice, but deep down, you do not give a shit. They will know, and in return, they will not give a shit.

At some point, you will need to get a job to be successful. Adults will most likely be in charge of giving you that position. When you go into the interview, you cannot say, "Yo, I am here for that position I saw in the paper on Sunday." Even if you are the most qualified for the job, your attitude is not going to get you through the first five minutes of the interview. Try this approach instead. *Example:* "Hello, Mr. Johnson. My name is Shaun. I am excited to be here interviewing for the position I saw in the paper on Sunday. As you can see, I am qualified for the job and feel I can be an asset to your company." Now, what is so hard about that? He or she may see that you are a nice individual who knows how to talk to people and offer you an even better position than the one you are applying for. All you did was use a little charm and you got the job. This is true in everything you do. Treat others with a little respect and see how the world around you changes. Doors will begin to open and opportunities will arise for you.

When I was younger, I would get enjoyment out of making adults unhappy. I felt that they were out to get me and I needed to strike first. I would try to embarrass them or make them look stupid in front of the other kids. This usually landed me in the principal's office. Meanwhile, everyone else was learning and I was just sitting in a chair doing shit. No wonder I never liked school. I didn't give myself a chance to learn anything. I was too busy pissing the people off who were trying to teach me. I look back now and try to figure out who I was impressing back then. Today, I only know one of the kids I went to grade school with. If I bumped into them now, they would not think I was cool. Old memories of that kid who always got in trouble would have been the impression I had left.

As we have discussed several times already in the book, nothing in this world is free. I hate to keep saying this, but it is true. Someone has to pay for things, even if at this point in your life, it is not you. As you get to become an adult yourself, your kids are going to come to you and ask for things. Do you want them to say to you, "Yo, get me that CD when you go to the store." No, of course not. At this point, you will have learned how hard it is to earn a dollar.

Adults need to be spoken to and approached much differently than you would approach your friends. Adults are usually under a lot of stress from their day-to-day activities already. They are usually tired and overworked. They do not need or deserve the kids in their lives to be disrespectful or rude to them. These are the most important people you have in your life. They will be there when your boys or girls are all gone. Here is an expression I like to describe what I mean: "Don't shit where you eat." Do not piss off the people you are close to. If you do, you will have no one but yourself. Some people feel they do not need anyone but themselves. These people are wrong and will be miserable throughout their lives.

Let's now look at ways to approach adults when something a little more serious is going on in your life. Example: You are going to meet some friends later today. These are friends that you have just recently met and think are really cool. You have hung out with them three times now and every time you are out, one of them breaks out a joint. They have never asked you to smoke it, but you think today that you may try it. You are scared and do not know what to do. This is a great example of a situation that you need to speak to an adult about. If you ask one of your friends to help you, the answer most likely will be what you want to hear and not what is in your best interests. This is definitely a tough question to build up the courage to ask an adult, but not a question that we will not understand. I would bet my life that there is not one adult in this country who does not understand that kids today are around drugs. If there are adults who do not understand this, tell me where they are and I will give them a good talking to. Approach the adult by saying, "I have something I need to talk about." Before you reveal what the question is, make sure you have their full attention. Turn off the TV or anything else distracting around them. Then start by saying, "I do not what you to get upset with me, but I need to ask you something and I want to be honest." Being honest about the question you are asking is very important. If you give only half the truth, you will only get half the answer. What is the point of that? If the adult begins to get upset when you ask this question, then you are talking to the wrong person. Do not get upset yourself. Just simply say thanks for their help and walk away. Do not get discouraged if this person did not try to understand your situation. This does not speak for most of us. Adults know kids need guidance and that is what we should be around to do. Move on until you find an adult whom you feel comfortable asking these types of questions. Make sure you trust this person and that they are not helping you for some other reason. This kind of help never should require you to do anything in return. It is free. I know better than anyone that part of growing up is just experimenting on your own and trying things without asking an adult first. But just remember to be very careful and think things through before making a serious decision of this kind.

Another very important way you can build your understanding with adults is simply by listening. When I say listening, I mean not saying anything all. Try not to argue but focus on what they are saying. I have learned more in my life by just listening to what others have to say about life. It does not mean I do exactly what I listen to. But I am able to hear what has worked for some people and what hasn't work for others. This gives me an advantage because someone has already been doing what I am interested in. It is like letting someone else steal the candy and you seeing what happens. Adults have experience in areas you have yet to explore. Let their knowledge be a useful guide to offer you many different approaches to a particular situation.

Let's begin to look at some very important situations that should be avoided when talking with people who are older than you. Adults should be there to help you. But, in this crazy fucked up world we live in, this is not always the case. Some adults are out to harm you. This process begins by an adult gaining your trust. They may do this by showing a strange interest in something that only kids should enjoy. They may start to buy you things, anything you want. Maybe they will buy you some cigarettes or alcohol even though you are not old enough to drink or smoke. Trust me when I say this: They are not doing this because they like to spend their money. They are trying to build your trust by giving you something most people would not. You start to think that this person is cool. They are hooking you up with smokes and booze. They will eventually want something in return. I can guarantee it is something that you are not going to be comfortable with. If you are involved in a relationship with an adult that you are not comfortable with, tell an adult you trust or your parents immediately. These types of situations will haunt you for the rest of your life. You are not old enough to understand now, but as you age, you will realize the importance of not growing up too fast. You have the rest of your life to be an adult. Right now, you need to focus on being a kid. Hang out with kids your same age and become involved in activities that your classmates are involved in. When you turn eighteen and twenty-one, then you will be old enough to make the decision whether or not you want to drink alcohol or smoke cigarettes. If you still feel the need to experiment, do so very cautiously and use your head at all times. If adults are pressuring you to try something you do not want to do, walk away and do not turn back. You are not missing anything by doing so.

The last point in this chapter I want to make clear: Treat your parents the way you want to be treated. Avoid swearing at them when things do not go your way. Think about how you feel when someone yells at you. You don't like it, and neither do your parents. You must remember, even when you are upset with a rule or decision your mother or father have made for you…they will still be the only parents you will ever have. You cannot trade them in for new ones. Your relationship with your parents will be the longest relationship in your life. Friends, girlfriends, boyfriends, teachers, and coaches will come and go, but your parents and family will always be with you. Right now, you may not understand how important it is to keep a positive relationship with your relatives, but as you get older, you will need these people to help you out in life. Do not push them away because you feel they do not let you do what you want to do. They are hard on you because they love you and want to see you safe and successful with everything you do in life. Oh...by the way, your parents brought you into this world. You should be the last person giving them any shit.

Dealing with problems

When I was younger, I was the worst at dealing with problems. All of the trouble I had gotten into was because I did not properly handle any of my problems. My biggest problem, dealing with my problems, is I didn't think I had any problems. If something went wrong in my life, I would try to blame anyone else other than myself. This was an easy way of not having to deal with anything. I would convince myself that everyone else was wrong and I was right. I chose not to take advice. I thought I had it all figured out. I didn't want anyone telling me how I should be living my life. Ultimately, what happened was my problems just kept getting worse and worse. I did not take care of my issues as they came; they began to pile up on top of one another. Pretty soon, I was in so much trouble I was taken out of my home at fourteen years old. At this point, I still thought everyone else was the one with the problems and not I. I am sure you all can relate to this way of dealing with things in your life. If you are doing poorly in school, it is because you hate your teachers. If you have been arrested, it was that asshole cop who screwed you over. One of the hardest parts of my job as a youth counselor is trying to get my students to admit that they are wrong. They would rather argue and lie about a problem for hours than admit they made a mistake. I do not blame them for this. I was the same way when I was younger. My kids would get caught smoking in the bathrooms and say that "I was playing them" when they got in trouble for it. If they were caught stealing, they would say, "Someone put his stuff in my locker to set me up." If they tested positive for smoking marijuana on a home pass, they would tell me that they were near someone who was smoking pot. By the way, just so you know, being around people who smoke pot does not make a drug screen positive. Only when you are sitting so close to them that you are inhaling the smoke will it make a drug test positive. Inhaling or possessing marijuana is illegal in the United States. It is no one's fault but your own if you get caught for marijuana charges. Maybe someday the laws on this will change, but until then, watch your ass. The point is, blaming others for your problems does not make them go away. If you do not accept the fact that you made a mistake, you will think you have done nothing wrong, therefore making no positive changes. It all comes back to responsibility. Being responsible and accepting responsibility for your actions is not something you change overnight. It takes you learning how to make responsible choices; in turn, you will become more responsible.

Making the best choice in a situation is what we need to focus on for a little while. The outcome of many situations can end up differently if the right choice was made in the beginning. Here's an example of what I like to call "a snowballing problem."

You wake up in the morning; it is time for you to get ready to go to school. While getting ready, you realize you did not do that easy five-minute homework assignment. You say to yourself "screw it" (Mistake #1). Next thing you know, you are on the bus to school. Your friends ask you if you did the math assignment. Of course you do not want to sound like a nerd so you say, "Hell no." Your friends reinforce your decision not to do the assignment by acting impressed (Mistake #2). By midday, you realize you are not going to get the assignment done. You become nervous about what the teacher may say to you when he/she asks you to turn it in (Mistake #3). The class arrives and the teacher asks you for the assignment. Of course you do not have it and he/she points out to the whole class that this is the tenth assignment you missed this month

(Mistake #4). As you are already nervous and on edge, you react by telling him/her, "I hate this fucking class anyway and don't give a shit!" (Mistake #5). She becomes very upset and sends you to the principal's office. You decide to keep up your nonsense, feeling as if you are already in trouble, so let's keep it going. You get to the office and decide to curse out the principal and walk off school grounds. The principal calls your family and tells them you are suspended for three days for leaving school grounds without permission, (Mistake #6). On the way home, you are so mad you walk into a convenience store and steal a magazine, (Mistake #7). The clerk sees you, (Mistake #8) no "just kidding." The clerk sees you and calls the police. You are picked up quickly down the street and arrested for shoplifting, (Mistake #9). At this point in the example, we have discovered many different times we could have stopped the problem from continuing to snowball. Let's look at each mistake and figure out what could have been done differently.

Mistake #1: Just do the five-minute assignment. Simple, I know a lot of us do not like to do what others tell us to do, but if we don't, we are the only ones who are going to suffer by it.

Mistake # 2: Just stop talking with your friends on the bus and do the assignment. They are not too concerned about it because they probably took the five minutes the night before to do it.

Mistake # 3: Just find some time and do the assignment. The reason you are feeling nervous about not having it done is because your body and mind sense trouble ahead if you do not turn it in. Trust your instincts; the voice inside your head is telling you to do the right thing. Just listen to it.

Mistake 4: Avoid blaming the teacher because you fail to hand in your work on time. He or she is trying to embarrass you so maybe next time you will do your work. Most likely, they would not have made a comment like that if they didn't care.

Mistake 5: Avoid continuing to take out your anger on the next person you see. They to do not deserve your attitude. The more people you piss off during the day, equals the more people that may be out to try and punish you.

Mistake 6: Do not feel that all is lost. Continuing to make more poor choices when we are upset does not make any of the original problems go away. When the smoke clears, every bad choice will need to be handled properly or go unresolved, leaving a negative lasting impression on those you hurt.

Mistake 7: At this point, we are in police custody and in some real serious shit. I know what you may be saying to yourself right now. "I do not handle my problems like that." You would be surprised how many people do. If you are not one of them, then you are off to a good start. Having the ability to accept responsibility for making a mistake will allow a problem to have an ending. You then move on and try to make a better choice in the future. If we had just taken the time out to do the assignment, we most likely would have not had the horrible day it turned into.

I watched a lot of the kids I counseled snowball problems. One of the hardest things about a snowballing problem is you do not know you are doing it because you are too mad to stop and think about what started the bad day. Some of my kids would have a small incident during breakfast, and by the end of the day, they would be shipped to a tougher facility. They allowed that minor breakfast ordeal to lead them to big trouble. I would like to also point out that there are people out there who enjoy watching others deal with their problems in the wrong way. These people sense that you are having a bad day and use your anger for their amusement. They may wait for the perfect time to say something mean to you so you start screaming and yelling at them, making yourself look more out of control than you already are. Be aware of this as well. Your friends may be hanging around sometimes because they want to see you act irresponsibly when it comes to dealing with problems. This way, they can get a cheap laugh while not getting in trouble themselves.

The next thing we should talk about when dealing with problems is accepting the fact that you are always going to have them. Everybody living on this planet has problems in one way or another. There is no avoiding them. There are just many different ways of handling them. The things you think are problems now will not be in five years. The problems you have five years from now will not concern you in ten. This cycle will continue throughout your life. It cannot be avoided. As you age, your priorities change. You will care about different things and your problems will reflect those issues. No one has the ability to master problem solving. A good problem-solver tries to completely understand a problem before attempting to solve it. This means not letting one's temper or attitude get in the way. This makes the problem harder to see. I am sure you have heard or seen something on the news where someone was killed over a parking space, or someone owed someone five dollars so they shot the other person. This seems completely crazy, right? Of course it is, but why do we still hear about things like this happening in our country? Easy, poor problem-solving techniques. These individuals want to solve the problem, whether it is getting the five dollars owed to them or parking their car where they wanted to. They just couldn't see the problem clearly and solved it in a way that was completely uncalled for. Their anger got in the way, clouding their judgment. When they calm down in a prison cell for the rest of their life for murder, they will most likely have thought of millions of different ways they could have handled that problem besides killing another human being over a stupid parking space or five dollars. Wouldn't it have been easier to just move the car to the next parking space, or forget about the five bucks and never lend that person money again?

I guess the point I am trying to make is, sit back for a second and try to think about what in your life is bothering you the most right now. Then think of the worst way you could resolve this problem and then think of the best way the problem can be solved. Now think of the consequences attached to handling the problem in the worst way, and do the same for the best way. Big difference, right? I bet handling the problem the worst way leads to a million more problems that are ten times worse than the problem you are trying to solve. Handling the problem the best way will most likely end the problem and not create another. Probably some of your problems you were thinking about are not really problems if you sit and think about them really hard. If something is bothering you and it is not really going to affect you at all, try and put that issue on the back burner for a while and concentrate on some problems that may affect you every day of your life. If you can clear up some of these major problems, this will give you more time to address these smaller ones that do not affect you so much but still bother you.

Another important thing about dealing with problems is not letting someone else's problems become your problems. Your friends may have asked you to help them solve a problem that has nothing even to do with you. This may not be a good idea due to the fact that this individual may not have taken the time to properly understand the problem, therefore, his solution could now cause unforeseen problems for both of you. This is not an easy thing to see coming. Where you need to stay sharp is asking yourself what are the benefits and consequences involved if I agree to help this individual with their problem. This goes back to the chapter we read surrounding peer pressure. Your friend may only be asking for help with this because he doesn't want to be the only one involved if something goes wrong. Use your own mind and think each situation through before just agreeing to give someone help.

I would like us to finish this chapter by examining one last point surrounding problems. Do not think at this point that you have just too many problems to deal with. Someone told me, "Hitting rock bottom is a good thing in life. This means all you can do is go up." This saying is true for all of us. Throughout our lives, we are going to have good times and bad. Sometimes, you may feel you don't have a care in the world. Other times, it may feel as if the whole world is out to get you, and no matter what changes you try to make, nothing seems to work. This is normal and will continue to happen. Problems will come and problems will be solved. At no time can you have too many problems that they cannot be fixed. If you feel this way, step back and try to look at your problems again. Clear your mind and try to take some small steps. Straightening out your life and future is not easy, but it can be done with time. I am sure you can remember a time you cared about something so much you put all your time into it. The same should be true for your life. Things just do not change because you want them to. You need to make a commitment to yourself and stick with it. Do not let friends or others steer you off the path of the goals you have set for yourself. Take small steps, achieving one goal at a time. Before long, you will see a brighter future ahead. Friends may change as you change. This sounds hard to deal with but it is natural. You begin to find that you have nothing in common with the kids who like to use drugs, skip school, sneak out at night, disobey their parents, do poorly in school, or even get arrested. At first, it will be difficult to leave these people because you may feel that getting in trouble is cool. But as you grow and mature, making the right choices in life, you will hopefully have learned that hurting your loved ones, failing out of school, using drugs, and maybe getting arrested is not cool. Some of your friends who do not grow up will not be around because they may have overdosed on drugs, been thrown in jail for a long time, or are homeless on the street because they have no education or job to support themselves with. Make sure you realize that when all the fun is over, you are going to have to exist on this planet one way or another. You can be prepared and ready to succeed or you can be unprepared and struggle to survive.

Thinking About Your Future

During this chapter, we will try to determine why it is so important to consider our future in every choice we make in life. First, your future is entirely up to you. Today's actions determine tomorrow's plan. If you make a mistake today, you may pay tomorrow. Securing a positive and happy future will depend on choices you make when you are too young to understand how they will affect your future. It is a huge burden to have to carry at such a young age, but that's the way our world is structured. We all cannot rewrite the past but the future is a blank page. What is written is up to you.

I would like to examine some major aspects in life you should be taking very seriously now to ensure you have a healthy future.

1. FAMILY

Family is very important to your future. Throughout your entire life, you need to count on your family for support and they count on you in return. It does not just go one way. You cannot always take from your family and give nothing back in return. At this point in your life, all you need to return is love and respect to those members of your family who give you love and respect. If you were to put down this book for a second and look around your room or look at the clothes on your back, most likely, your family has a lot to do with it, right? I am sure you are not making enough money right now to afford the new Nike sneakers or PlayStation video game system. Your family feeds, clothes, and buys you things so you stay happy and enjoy life. I understand that these things may not make everyone happy, but still it does not mean that they should be taken for granted. People today work very hard for their money. Just the fact that they spend it on you shows they want to give you what you need in life. Have you ever seen your relatives walk down the street and give everybody that walks by a twenty-dollar bill? No, of course not. They have no connection to those people and they want to see their money help their loved ones, like you. You should take advantage of the time you have with your family now. As you get older, you will eventually move out of your family's house and into your own house or apartment. You spend less time with your family. The support they give you also becomes less. Once out on your own, it is up to you to put the sneakers on your feet, clothes on your back, and food in your mouth. Your family will continue to be there for you, but not the same way as when you were a kid. If, during your childhood and teenage years, you spend your family time telling them how much you hate them and the stupid rules they set down for you, time will be lost arguing and fighting instead of enjoying each others' lives together. As you grow, building your relationships now will avoid them spreading apart until eventually you may not talk with family all that much. It won't be because you don't like your family but because you do not know your family. You were too busy trying to stay away from them, so they didn't see what kind of negative things you were really up to. Be a positive member of your family now…..YOUR FUTURE DEPENDS ON IT.

2. EDUCATION

Education, Education, Education. I cannot stress this fact enough. It is the one thing in life that no one can take from you. The knowledge in your head defines who, what, and where you will end up in life. It is one of the hardest things for you to understand right now because when you are learning, you rarely see rewards you can touch. Your education is worth more than any other thing you own, if you can see its worth towards your future.

Let me put it this way...if I asked you right now to go outside with a pair of scissors and cut every blade of grass in your yard one by one, you would most likely tell me to go to hell. It would be boring, dirty, time-consuming, pointless, and not much fun at all. This is the kind of job you can look forward to for the rest of your life if you have no education. This does not make you stupid, it is just in the category of the kind of work you will fit into. Think it about. You are at a job interview. It is your dream position, let's say working for MTV promoting their station around the world. Of course you are not going to be the only one applying for this job. As you look around the waiting room, there are many people your age. You think to yourself, hey, these people look a lot like me. I have just as good a chance of getting this job as the next guy. When you go into the interview, the person hiring loves your personality. Then they ask you what you studied in school. If you cannot give them some educational background, they will immediately judge you as someone who cannot finish things completely. The job will eventually go to the person who is qualified for the job educationally. Your education is your mark on how determined you are to succeed in life. Knowledge you gain in books and in the classroom can be used to help you understand the world around you. The type of job you have, car you drive, house you live in, friends you hang with, and life you live depends on getting the proper education now. A few more years of studying for a lifetime of enjoyable work sounds like a pretty good deal. Take your education seriously...YOUR FUTURE DEPENDS ON IT.

3. HEALTH

Taking care of health now will determine how well your body performs in the future. There are many ways you can risk your health at a young age. Smoking cigarettes and using drugs will affect your body's growth and development. These substances are not natural and do not belong inside our bodies. At a young age, you are able play and run around all day. As you continue to abuse the body with chemicals, your lungs and other parts of the body are affected. Soon, you will have trouble breathing. The simple task of running 500 feet will feel as if you ran ten miles. You also need to be aware of the food you are eating. A junk food diet may taste good, but it does not provide all the vitamins and energy the body needs to stay healthy. Exercising regularly and eating a balanced meal will give you more energy throughout the day and keep your brain thinking clearly. Do not deprive yourself of sleep. A tired body and mind does not function properly, therefore, making learning and listening much more difficult. Avoid engaging in high-risk activities. If a friend wants to go cliff jumping into a shallow river, think about how it would feel to break both of your legs if you hit the bottom. Breaking bones and injuring yourself will affect your body negatively throughout your life. I am not trying to say avoid having fun, just remember to take into consideration that you have only one body. Treat it with some care… YOUR FUTURE DEPENDS ON IT.

4. NO CRIMINAL RECORD

Avoid a criminal record at all costs. My adult criminal record has closed so many doors for me in my life it is unbelievable. A criminal record is permanent. As you grow, this part of your past grows with you. It is a public record anyone can view to see how you behaved when you were younger. If you happen to become convicted of a felony charge, your rights as a citizen are taken away forever. You will not be allowed to vote, hold a gun (that's no big deal: guns kill people), join the military, be selected for jury duty, or get a good job. Every time you fill out a job application, there will be this nice little section that asks if you "Have ever been convicted of a felony?" It then says, "Please explain. This will not necessarily exclude you from this position." That is a bunch of bullshit. If that were not going to exclude you from the position, why ask the question in the first place? Any charge you are convicted of as an adult can be thrown back in your face for any reason at any time. Do not give society this ammunition to use against you. It is not worth it. Play by the rules. There are a million activities you can do that are legal. Avoid the law...YOUR FUTURE DEPENDS ON IT.

5. CHOOSE YOUR FRIENDS WISELY

Choosing your friends will determine what type of activities you become involved with. If you decide to hang around with a bunch of kids who play sports, you will most likely spend a lot of time playing sports. If you hang with musicians, you will play music. If you are around kids who take school seriously, your grades will improve. If you are always around kids using drugs, you will use drugs. Hang with kids who vandalize the town, you to will eventually vandalize the town. It is simple. The direction you want to go in life will be determined by the friends you keep. It goes back to trusting your instincts. I am sure everyone knows the kid in town whom parents do not want their kids to hang out with. They are saying it for a reason. They know if you hang around with the bad kid in town, before long, you will be in trouble, too. I am sure you have said to a friend, "My parents would kill me if they knew we were hanging out." Troublemakers like hearing about their negative reputations throughout the town. It is the attention he is trying to obtain by acting so badly. You reinforce it by saying that to him. Now he has to live up to his reputation by showing you just how negative he can be. The problem is he is not going to say, "Hey, you stay here and watch me get arrested." He is going to make sure you are with him or her to take the fall as well. If you are hanging with a kid you are not supposed to be, stop hanging with that kid. YOUR FUTURE DEPENDS ON IT.

6. MONEY

A sad fact in the world today is we need money to do anything. There is not too much left that costs nothing. Enjoying nature, exercising outdoors, or just hanging out with someone you love can still be done at no cost to you, but the majority of what you need to survive costs cash. You will most likely spend the rest of your life trying to make as much money as possible to survive. In today's economy, we all need a lot of it, while money is harder to come by than ever. Jobs are few and highly competitive. More and more individuals are college educated. A lot of American companies are sending their factories overseas to save money on salaries. This is all going on while we are led to live in constant fear of terrorist attacks. I do not want to get political, but I do want to make it clear; it is tough going out in the world today. You should begin to have some thoughts about what you would do in the future to make money. I do not mean you need to know exactly what you want to be when you get older. If you do have some idea, you could start now by gaining as much knowledge about that subject as you can. This will make you prepared for your financial road ahead. It also is a good idea to begin to learn how to save a dollar or two. You could also spend some time learning how money works and how investments operate. Putting some money in the proper place now will ease financial strain for your future. Even if you get a little savings account, your money will be working for you by gaining interest. Interest is free money the bank gives us for depositing our money with their company. It may not be much, but every penny we get for free is more than we had before, and we didn't have to work for it.

As we get older, the amount of money needed to get by increases. Pretty soon, twenty dollars will not be that much anymore. If they do not have a good source of income, some people choose to get their money through criminal activities. Most criminal acts revolve around money. People need money to live. If they have no legal way of getting any money, crime seems to be the solution. Well, the old saying goes "Crime doesn't pay." If you decide to use crime as a means of getting money, it may work for a while. But sooner or later, everyone gets caught. Next thing you know, you have no clothes, only an orange jumpsuit and big scary prison roommate. For what? A little bit of extra cash. If you had a full-time job, you would see far more money in the long haul and you would never need to worry about meeting the prison roommate. Having no money is not in your best interest. Without money to survive, even people who normally are not criminals become desperate and may do something against the law to get what they need. Be prepared for a future of making money and you will be too busy to get caught up in the all the other bullshit...YOUR FUTURE DEPENDS ON IT.

7. STAY INFORMED

Staying informed is the least you can do for yourself. What I mean is try and watch the news or read a newspaper every once in a while. Learn about the country you live in. Have some ideas of what you think is right or wrong and make your own conclusions about what should be done. Learning about your culture will open your mind and give you current knowledge about what's happening around you. Some day, you may be the one making decisions that affect others. The more informed you are to make those the decisions, the better off we all are.

I try to watch the news every day. I find it very interesting because it is supposed to be the truth and may affect me directly. Unlike most other television programs that are made up, in which no matter what happens at the end, it will not change our lives, the world has changed a lot over the past couple of years. If we do not stay in tune with what is going on, we will wake up to find our country has changed in ways we were unaware of at the time and, therefore, did nothing about. There is another old saying, "Ignorance is bliss." This is only good for those who are counting on us to be uninformed. This way, people in power can make choices that directly affect everyone with little argument. If we were all properly informed, some decisions may not be as easy to pass. Try and keep up with current events...YOUR FUTURE DEPENDS ON IT.

8. DON'T SPEND TO MUCH TIME WORRYING ABOUT YOUR FUTURE

Even though there is a lot to consider about the future, be sure to enjoy the present. As time goes on, you will make these decisions when the time is right for you. Worrying about all these things at once will only make you miserable. Things happen for a reason. Your life will be determined by the people you meet and choices and mistakes you make. Learn from the past and try to be prepared for the future. Great things may be in store for you down the road. Be sure you are in the right position to take advantage if a once-in-a-lifetime opportunity comes your way...YOUR FUTURE DEPENDS ON IT.

Being Happy with Yourself

Ahh....The last chapter. I bet you are saying to yourself, "Good, I never thought this loser would shut-up." Well, all you need to do is get through this last one and you will have finished another book, a great accomplishment. This chapter is going to deal with being happy with you. This is so important in life. Everywhere we turn, someone or something is telling us we need to get this or we need that to fit in. If you don't have the latest style or listen to the most popular music you are not "in". This is done for a reason. Companies want to make you keep buying new stuff, even if you do not need it. Media achieves this goal very well by constantly putting out the image of what the perfect girl should look like and what the perfect guy should look like. Very few of us will ever look like either of these people. That's fine, I do not want to look like someone else. I want to look like me. Don't you? Each and every one of us is unique in our own way. If every girl and guy looked like someone on a magazine cover or poster, I think we would be a pretty boring bunch of so-called good-looking people.

Major companies use these images to sell you products. They want you to always feel ugly so you go out and buy something to make you think you look better. Once everyone has bought this new product and the company has made a lot of MONEY, they turn around and say it is out of style. Next, you will need to get this now. The cycle goes on and on this way. Being in style is wearing what you want to wear. You have the option of wearing what you think is cool, and what makes you happy when you are in it. Don't worry if someone else doesn't like it; you can't please everyone. The only reason they would take the time to make fun of it anyway is because they probably like what you're wearing but are too afraid to wear it themselves. So instead, they try to make you feel stupid. Think about it. Why would anyone really care what you are wearing? Is it affecting them any bit at all? No. Most styles are not styles at first. It always takes those individuals who don't give a shit what others think to develop a current style. Wear what you want and do not let others tell you what is in or what isn't. You have your own brain, and you determine what you think.

Today's youth, and most likely kids in the past, have always used overweight people as a target for ridicule. Being overweight is not the end of the world. Some people's bodies just burn off what is eaten during activity. Others tend to hang on to what they eat and it shows physically. This does not mean you eat too much or you are lazy. It means we are different, our bodies are different. Some people are tall; some short. Blue eyes, brown eyes, blond hair, black hair, big body, tiny body, you are made up of your genes. This is your body's map. You are not in control and they cannot be changed. What you are in control of is how you treat your body, both physically and mentally. If a person does not take care themselves, it does not matter how much they weigh. A person's weight does not completely determine health. If magazine covers always had pictures of overweight people on them, every tiny girl and guy I know would be stuffing their faces with Big Macs. It is silly, but true. Society defines beauty, beauty defines style, and style equals money. If someone calls you fat, you tell them, "Hey, at least I can lose weight, but you can't change that ugly face of yours." See what they say to that. No one has the right to make fun of your body. No one is perfect, because we do not even know what perfect is.

In order to be happy with ourselves, we need to be involved in activities and surroundings that make us happy. Sports, friends, family, hobbies, music, or spending time in your favorite place are excellent ways to build your spirit. Try not to spend all your time on the same activity. A wide variety of activities will keep your brain stimulated. If you choose to spend eight hours a day in front of the TV, your mind will go numb from boredom. Try and avoid fixating all your energy on your girlfriend or boyfriend. At this point in your life, taking a relationship too seriously is not a good idea. You will meet many more people down the road who may be more compatible. Use your time to explore life and explore new things. Trying new things is an excellent way to see what you are good at and what you may prefer not to do. If you do not try something once, how do know whether or not it is for you? You could be the greatest soccer player that ever lived, but you won't know unless you try. Don't worry if you do something for the first time and suck at it. Practice makes perfect in almost everything we do. Give yourself the opportunity to push your body and test its limits.

When I think back to my teenage years, I was always unhappy. I cannot even tell you now why this was. I guess I was just pissed off at the world. I would look at everything with a negative point of view. I thought nothing I did was right and everyone was out to get me. As I got older and my attitude became more positive, I started to see things in a different light. People were nicer to me and I started to enjoy each day I was alive. I now realize that when I was younger, I treated everyone like shit. In turn, people treated me like shit. Our attitude is everything. If we begin to cheer up and take things as they come in a calm manner, problems will get solved and life will move on. Staying happy and positive makes life much easier to digest.

I would like to finish my book by saying I enjoyed the time we spent together. I understand that you are not going to agree with everything I said in the book. I did not write this to try and change who you are or what you think. I wrote the book as a guide you could use to help ease the stress of being young and living on this confusing planet. Hopefully, I may have answered some questions you were afraid to ask others about. I am not saying I know everything, far from it. I do know that when I was a kid, I did not think I would see my twenty-first birthday. But here I am, twenty-six. I had a long journey to make it to this point. I would not change the way I lived my life up to this point for the world. Growing up in environments where everything is not handed to you is good. It builds strength and character. You will be strong in the future and able to achieve your goals. Do not be ashamed of where you come from, the color of your skin, how you talk, or how much money you have. We all go to sleep under the same stars each night.

Peace and Love,

Jay!

Printed in the United States
91119LV00004BA/520-549/A